Praise for
The Emotionally Destru

T0190620

"This book is a lifeline for women who long to live a Christ-honoring life but are caught in the downward spiral of a destructive relationship. Leslie draws from a deep well of biblical insight, practical experience, and courageous advocacy to give individuals and the church the tools necessary to set captives free—one woman at a time."

—Joe Henseler, senior pastor of Faith Evangelical Free Church, Allentown, Pennsylvania

"As a radio host, I regularly hear from women who feel trapped in destructive marriages. Because they hear God hates divorce, they don't know what they can do. Leslie shows them exactly what they can do in this book. It's packed with solid, practical, and biblical steps to get sane, get safe, and get strong."

—Anita Lustrea, author, speaker, and host of Moody Radio's *Midday Connection*

"Though marriage is God's idea, many marriages are not being lived out according to God's plan. Leslie skillfully takes the reader through specific check points, uncovering relationships that are destructive while giving valuable tools for genuine healing. This book will point many couples in the direction of change and discovery of God's ultimate plan of mutual respect and love."

—Ray and Debbie Alsdorf, authors of *Beyond the Brady Bunch*

"The *Emotionally Destructive Marriage* blows the lid off the silence surrounding this serious epidemic in the church. It's packed with the kind of solid practical wisdom and bracing straight talk women need to face reality and engage safely the crisis in their marriage. Every Christian leader should read this eyeopening corrective to damaging advice often coming from the church to women in abusive marriages. Women who are at the end of their rope will find this book to be an invaluable lifeline."

—CAROLYN CUSTIS JAMES, author of *The Gospel of Ruth* and *Half the Church*

"This book provides answers and action for women who are caught in the vicious cycle of emotional abuse. Kudos to Leslie Vernick for addressing and exposing this prevalent problem head on and offering her wise counsel to hurting women."

—SUELLEN ROBERTS, founder and president of Christian Women in Media

"The *Emotionally Destructive Marriage* is the perfect tool for pastors, counselors, and marriage leaders to help women caught in destructive marriages. Written with a softness that only Leslie Vernick could deliver but with a tenacity to motivate and help women recognize their plight, this book provides the practical insights they need to step into the emotional and relational freedom they deserve."

—JOSHUA STRAUB, PHD, coauthor of *God Attachment*

"Women in an emotionally abusive marriage do not need another book on how to have a good marriage; those books rub salt in raw wounds. No, they desperately need this book so that they can diagnose just how bad their marriage is and then, with Leslie's clear expertise, develop a plan that will either begin to turn their marriage around, strengthen them to stay and survive, or give them a wise route of escape. I was riveted from the first chapter and thanked God repeatedly for this clear manual for those who are in such need of a lifeline."

—DEE BRESTIN, author of *Idol Lies* and *The Friendships of Women*

"*The Emotionally Destructive Marriage* extends a lifeline of well-tested, biblically sound, practical, real help to women who are often at the end of their rope, end of their ability to cope, and end of their hope. Leslie's common-sense wisdom and tender encouragement might help save your marriage, your family, and your future—and it will for sure save your sanity, your life, and your heart. Every leader, and every woman, needs copies to hand out."

—PAM FARREL, author of *The 10 Best Decisions a
Woman Can Make* and *Men Are Like Waffles;
Women Are Like Spaghetti*

"This book is a significant contribution to Christian literature on the subject of abuse in marriage. Into church cultures so often clouded by a fog of confusion and unbiblical tradition, Leslie's words shine a welcome light. She understands the mentality and nature of abuse that drives these emotionally destructive marriages. I intend to put her book to use in our church in both women's and men's groups, and I would encourage Bible colleges and seminaries to do the same."

—JEFF CRIPPEN, pastor and author of *A Cry for Justice:
How the Evil of Domestic Abuse Hides in Your Church*

"Leslie's book tackles a hidden epidemic behind the closed doors of many Christian homes. Leslie provides help—winsome yet tough, practical yet immensely biblical help—for those in destructive marriages. Counselors, pastors, and Christian ministry leaders are given a clear compass to know how to take a marriage from broken to whole, if both individuals are willing to work."

—TIM CLINTON, PhD, president of the American Association
of Christian Counselors and executive director of the Center
for Counseling and Family Studies at Liberty University

"Heart-to-heart reality checkup. Destructive myths and assumptions exposed. Marriages advanced. Women valued. Hopeful steps for real change. That's how Leslie Vernick writes to women who are under attack in marriage. She provides fresh God-honoring solutions as she speaks life-changing truth for women. Her honesty and mandates for frustrated or failed marriage relationships are invigorating, incredible, practical, and based on the Bible."

—ROGER BALL, senior pastor of First Baptist of Tempe

"Finally, a voice being put to the very real problem of emotional abuse within a marriage and the invisible wounds it inflicts on the spirit, heart, and mind. Leslie Vernick brings light to the breakdown that happens in a relationship marked by toxic behavior. Her years of wisdom and expertise in this area, along with her biblical insight, are to be applauded. Thank you, Leslie, for being an advocate for freedom."

—MICHELLE BORQUEZ, president of God Crazy Freedom, author of *Overcoming the Seven Deadly Emotions*

"We like to think that every marriage can be repaired and fully restored, but that's not reality in this fallen world. Kudos to Leslie Vernick for being one of the first to address this reality. I'll be recommending this book to many coaching clients in the coming years, because within these pages they'll discover so many valuable assets. I particularly love how she teaches women four steps to develop CORE strength, which helps them deal with their destructive partner in truth and with grace."

—SHANNON ETHRIDGE, MA, relationship coach, speaker, and best-selling author of *Every Woman's Battle*

LESLIE VERNICK

How to
Find Your Voice
and Reclaim
Your Hope

The
Emotionally
Destructive
Marriage

- Moving Toward Healing
- Deciding Whether to Stay or Go
- Breaking Free from Damaging Patterns

WATERBROOK

THE EMOTIONALLY DESTRUCTIVE MARRIAGE

All Scripture quotations, unless otherwise indicated, are taken from The Holy Bible, English Standard Version, copyright © 2001 by Crossway Bibles, a division of Good News Publishers. Used by permission. All rights reserved. Scripture quotations marked (NIV) are taken from the Holy Bible, New International Version®, NIV®. Copyright © 1973, 1978, 1984 by Biblica Inc.™ Used by permission of Zondervan. All rights reserved worldwide. www.zondervan.com. Scripture quotations marked (NKJV) are taken from the New King James Version®. Copyright © 1982 by Thomas Nelson Inc. Used by permission. All rights reserved. Scripture quotations marked (NLT) are taken from the Holy Bible, New Living Translation, copyright © 1996, 2004, 2007. Used by permission of Tyndale House Publishers Inc., Carol Stream, Illinois 60188. All rights reserved.

Italics in Scripture quotations reflect the author's added emphasis.

Details in some anecdotes and stories have been changed to protect the identities of the persons involved.

Trade Paperback ISBN 978-0-307-73118-0
eBook ISBN 978-0-307-73119-7

Copyright © 2013 by Leslie Vernick

Cover design by Kelly L. Howard; cover photo by Ben Welsh, Corbis

Published in the United States by WaterBrook, an imprint of the Crown Publishing Group, a division of Penguin Random House LLC, New York.

WATERBROOK® and its deer colophon are registered trademarks of Penguin Random House LLC.

Library of Congress Cataloging-in-Publication Data
Vernick, Leslie.
    The emotionally destructive marriage : how to find your voice and reclaim your hope / Leslie Vernick.
        pages cm
    Includes bibliographical references.
    ISBN 978-0-307-73118-0 — ISBN 978-0-307-73119-7
    1. Marriage—Religious aspects—Christianity. 2. Emotions—Religious aspects—Christianity. I. Title.
    BV835.V47 2013
    248.8'44—dc23
                                                                2013014766

Printed in the United States of America

20th Printing

SPECIAL SALES
Most WaterBrook books are available at special quantity discounts when purchased in bulk by corporations, organizations, and special-interest groups. Custom imprinting or excerpting can also be done to fit special needs. For information, please e-mail specialmarketscms@penguin randomhouse.com or call 1-800-603-7051.

Contents

To the bravest women I know.
Your faith, strength, and courage inspire me.

Acknowledgments

Birthing a book always involves a long, painful labor. I grunt and groan, writhe, and scream out for help. I am so grateful for those who faithfully prayed for me during my labor pains. Many times, total strangers would e-mail me or message me that I was in their prayers. I don't know your names, but I want you to know that without you this book would not have been born.

Those who were close by held my hand, made my meals, and rubbed my shoulders when I felt hunched over from writing so much. My husband, Howard, is my hero. He cooked meals for me and lovingly brought me my morning tea. When I feared I was gaining weight from too much sitting, he rigged up a table on my treadmill so I could write while walking, breaking up the long stretches of sitting. My friend Barb graciously allowed me space and time to write at her beach house while we were supposed to be having fun. My son, Ryan, often tended other house chores that I just was too busy or distracted to take care of. Meanwhile my daughter, Amanda, had some real babies of her own who brought joy to my heart.

I'd also like to thank my dear friend Dee Brestin for sitting with me at her dining room table, encouraging me to write what no one wants to talk about or face. Georgia Shaffer, Paula Silva, and Ginny Yttrup, thank you for graciously reading through the first draft of my manuscript and giving me your wise and helpful feedback. Bill Watkins, thank you for your meticulous biblical scholarship helping me understand biblical covenant and a larger picture of marriage and divorce. My office manager, Donna Barats, thank you for faithfully keeping my schedule, gathering my loose ends, and documenting all my endnotes—in addition to everything else you do—so that I could focus on writing. Susan Tjaden, my editor, you made my manuscript a much better book. Thank you for all your efforts. To my publisher, WaterBrook Multnomah, I am deeply appreciative for your believing in the importance of this topic and publishing this book. I am also grateful to the men and women who have allowed me to walk beside them in their shattered lives and marriages. You have taught me so much.

Lastly, God, without you I would have nothing to say. You hate injustice and abuse, and it breaks your heart to see it happening within families and in your church. Thank you for giving me the privilege of speaking up for those who cannot speak for themselves.

Hanging On by a Thread

It's easy to find a plethora of good books about how to be a godly wife or what steps to take to build a successful and happy marriage. There aren't many books written on how to wisely deal with a destructive and abusive marriage. As a counselor and coach, I have grown increasingly troubled by the advice hurting women receive from well-meaning pastors, Christian counselors, friends, and lay leaders when they seek help for their destructive and abusive marriages. Many times we've not understood the gravity of the problem. We've misdiagnosed a marriage that has terminal cancer and treated it as if it were only suffering from a common cold. We've also misplaced the responsibility for keeping the marriage alive by putting an extraordinarily heavy burden on a wife's shoulders to somehow maintain a loving and warm relationship with a husband who treats her with cruelty, disrespect, deceit, and gross indifference. It's not feasible, nor is it biblical.

Each week e-mails flood my inbox from women desperate for answers, hanging on to their marriages and sometimes their sanity by a single thread. The details vary, but the questions are usually the same: "What do I do?" and "Where do I turn for help?" The woman's spirit, and sometimes her body, is depressed and depleted from the distress she feels within the walls of her own home. She wants to honor God and do his will, but does that mean she must continue to allow herself to be destroyed by her husband, a man who has promised to love and protect her?

Marriage and family are important to God, but just as important to him are the individuals within those marriages and families. God does not value men more than women, or the institution of marriage more than the people who are in it. He wants to help you know how to heal and what to do to bring true restoration to your destructive marriage. He also knows that because of the hardness of your husband's heart, true reconciliation of your relationship isn't always possible.

Throughout this book you will clearly see what's wrong and why keeping the marriage together at all costs or at any price can be dangerous. You will gain fresh insights and a new paradigm in which to understand your role in your marriage. You'll learn strategies and be given tools so that you can find your own voice again and be able to develop the strength and courage to stand up against the destruction. Within these pages is a biblical road map to help you know whether genuine repentance and restoration is taking place, and what the specific steps are to get there.

The Emotionally Destructive Marriage is divided into three parts. Part 1, "Seeing Your Marriage Clearly," will help you distinguish the difference between a disappointing marriage and a destructive one. At the end of chapter 1, there is a self-administered test you can take to determine whether you are in a destructive marriage. In chapter 2 you will learn what a healthy marriage looks like and the three essential ingredients that are required for any relationship to flourish. Chapter 3 will open your eyes to the different types of destructive relationship patterns and why they are so damaging to you, your children, and your marriage. In chapter 4 you will see that God hates what's happening to you. He is with you and for you and wants to help you make changes so that genuine healing can take place.

Part 2, "Change Begins with You," opens with chapter 5 showing you the ways you may be unknowingly enabling the destruction in your marriage to continue. You will understand how being a true biblical helpmate is very different than staying inappropriately submissive and silent about the destruction. In chapter 6 you'll understand why trying harder in the traditional wifely ways will make a destructive marriage worse and how the common teachings on biblical headship and submission can lead to an abuse of power and entitlement thinking. Chapter 7 will help you build internal core strength, so that when the time is right, you will be empowered to take firm yet godly action to protect yourself and your children. Then, in chapter 8, you will know exactly what you need to do to prepare before you have a difficult conversation with your husband about his destructive behaviors.

In part 3, "Initiating Changes in Your Marriage," you'll be given specific strategies to wake up your husband to his destructiveness and invite him to godly change. In chapter 9 you'll discover how to speak up in love, using words that invite your spouse to stop his destructive behaviors and attitudes without shaming, scolding, or disrespecting him. In chapter 10 you will receive a plan on how to calmly confront your husband, together with examples of specific consequences you can implement if he refuses to listen. Chapter 11 takes you step by step through your biblical options if nothing changes in your marriage, and ways you can stay strong and God-centered in the midst of continued destructive behaviors. Lastly, in chapters 12 and 13, you'll learn the specific changes that are required if a destructive marriage is to heal, and how you will know whether or not you're making progress as a couple. In the closing epilogue, I invite you to read the words of an abusive man who is learning to become a better man.

I debated whether to write this book just for women or to include men, as they, too, are in destructive marriages and feel distraught, impotent, and confused about how to change the damaging dynamics in their marriages. In the end I decided to write this book for women, but if you are a man who is looking for answers for your destructive marriage, you will find help within the pages here if you can overlook the stories and illustrations depicting men as the primary perpetrators. You can also find additional resources at www.leslievernick.com/the-emotionally-destructive -marriage, if your wife is the one who is the destructive partner.

The individuals in each story are disguised except for those who have given me permission to use their real names. Some stories or characters are composites to illustrate a specific point. All are pictures of the painful realities some women must live with day after day, week after week, year after year.

Please hear me: God doesn't want you to hang on by a thread, my friend. He gives you a lifeline. Grab hold of it and live.

PART 1

Seeing Your Marriage Clearly

The eye is the lamp of the body. So, if your eye is healthy, your whole body will be full of light, but if your eye is bad, your whole body will be full of darkness. If then the light in you is darkness, how great is the darkness!

Jesus, in Matthew 6:22–23

One

Are You in an Emotionally Destructive Marriage?

For nothing is hidden except to be made manifest;
nor is anything secret except to come to light.

—Mark 4:22

Several years ago, while speaking in Hungary, I was shocked to see the new title the Hungarians had given one of my books when they translated it into their language. It was now called *How to Survive a D-Minus Marriage*. My sister, Patt, who had accompanied me on this speaking trip, joked with me about whether or not people would admit their marriages were that bad. But during the event, the book sold like hot cakes. Marriages everywhere are in dire straits. Christian homes are no exception.

You may feel as if you are in a D-minus marriage and have no idea what to do. I have help for you, but first it's important to clarify the difference between a disappointing marriage and a destructive one.

A DISAPPOINTING MARRIAGE

Anna perched on the edge of her chair, her hands folded neatly in her lap. When I asked her to tell me why she'd come to see me, tears sprung to her eyes. Embarrassed, she grabbed a tissue and dabbed her lashes so her mascara wouldn't run. "I don't know why I'm crying," Anna stammered, her lip trembling. "I should be happy. I have a great life. My husband is good with the girls, generously provides for our family, and is overall a nice guy."

"So what's the problem?" I asked.

"I guess I thought we'd have more of a connection. I don't feel that spark for him. I don't know if I ever did. And…maybe…I wonder if I had waited, I could I have done better. Now I dread the thought of spending the rest of my life with him."

As Anna and I talked, I learned she grew up in a tumultuous home filled with chaos and conflict. When she met Mark, he personified stability, strength, and security—something Anna never experienced growing up. Mark was a committed Christian, which in Anna's mind made him magnificent husband material. She loved being taken care of and feeling safe, but she hadn't considered some of his other qualities like his reserved nature, his quietness, and his lack of adventure. And now, although she's snug and secure, she feels lonely, bored, and trapped.

Anna's marriage is not destructive, but it is disappointing and painful for her. She's not sure how to continue or even if she wants to. Yet she knows to end her marriage for these reasons would crush Mark and her children, as well as dishonor her vows to God and to her husband. Anna feels vulnerable and confused and miserable. She wants to trust God, and yet she desperately wants to be happy in a great relationship. She can't imagine having that with Mark.

A DESTRUCTIVE MARRIAGE

Like Anna, Carol was miserable in her marriage but for completely different reasons. Carol was pacing back and forth in my office, her mascara smeared from crying, desperate for answers.

"Leslie, I don't know how to live this way anymore. My husband tells me I'm fat, worthless, and lazy. He mocks me and makes fun of me when I cry or get mad. I don't know what to do when he tells the children they don't have to listen to me or that I'm too stupid to help them with their homework. And sex! I'm not even going to go there, but let me just say this much, if I'm not interested, I have to listen to how screwed up I am or how every woman would love to do the things he wants to do.

"I've gone to my pastor for help, and although he seems sympathetic, all he tells me is to trust God and try harder to submit and love my husband. I feel crazy inside. I already know God says I'm supposed to submit. But how? How do I submit to someone who is irresponsible with our money? How do I submit to someone who acts like he hates me? How do I feel any kind of love for a man who emotionally batters me and sexually degrades me?"

I said, "You can't."

"I can't?" Carol stopped pacing and sunk down into a chair, her eyes riveted on mine.

I smiled. "You can't. You are in a living nightmare. You're not wrong for feeling angry and hurt. God hates the way your husband treats you. It's evil."

"Then what do I do?" Carol asked.

"Carol, it is impossible to love your husband in a warm and wifely way right now, but God does want you to love him, even if he feels like your enemy. What this kind of love looks like in your situation is something we'll work on together. However, I want you to hear this important truth. Biblically loving your husband doesn't require you to prop him up in order to enable him to continue to hurt you. It involves something far more redemptive."

Like Anna, Carol is in a D-minus marriage. But Carol's relationship isn't just disappointing; it is destructive. Her husband not only hurts her feelings, but he consistently degrades her personhood and devalues her voice. He rejects her as a biblical helpmate and uses her as an object to meet his sexual desires. His actions and attitudes toward Carol are not just sinful; they are destructive. They tear her down and inhibit her growth. This is toxic not only to Carol but also to him as a man and to their children who observe how their father treats their mother day in and day out. (In chapter 3, I'll describe additional attitudes and behaviors that are destructive to the marriage and to the individuals in them.)

> Biblically loving your husband doesn't require you to prop him up in order to enable him to continue to hurt you. It involves something far more redemptive.

Carol's unhappiness and Anna's unhappiness are for different reasons, but God cherishes both women and their families. Anna is not in a destructive marriage, but she is in a disappointing one. In our feel-good and entitlement culture, more and more Christian men and women are abandoning their marriages for the simple reason that "I want more" or "I'm not happy." Anna's unhappiness is like a sore in her soul that she must tend to if she wants it to heal. If she continues to pick at it, it will become inflamed—perhaps infected—and will affect her marriage and her whole person. Her unhappiness could become destructive if she acts out by having an affair or divorcing her husband simply because she's lonely or bored.

Every marriage goes through seasons of closeness and separateness, happy times and hard times. After thirty-eight years of marriage to the same man and more than thirty-five years of counseling hundreds of couples, I've learned that good marriages don't just happen, even if partners were madly in love when they first got married. It is in marriage, more than any other relationship, where we come face to face with the best in ourselves and the absolute worst in ourselves, as well as the best and the worst in our spouse. How we do—or do not—face this awareness and respond to it becomes the running theme of our marital and personal story and will determine the success or failure of our marriage, and much of our life.

What Is Emotional Abuse?

Whenever I do a radio or television interview on the topic of emotionally destructive relationships, the moderator always says something like, "We all do hurtful things at times to people. We all make mistakes and do or say things we regret. When is the line crossed? When does it become destructive? How do you define emotional abuse?"

Emotional abuse systematically degrades, diminishes, and can eventually destroy the personhood of the abused. Most people describe emotional abuse as being far more painful and traumatic than physical abuse. One only has to read reports of prisoners of war to begin to understand the traumatic effects of psychological warfare using emotionally abusive tactics—and this is when the behavior is perpetrated by one's enemy. When the abusive behavior is perpetrated by someone who promises to love and cherish you, it is even more devastating and destructive.

Destructive behaviors and attitudes can sometimes be difficult to describe succinctly. That's why an emotionally destructive marriage is not usually diagnosed by looking at a single episode of sinful behavior (which we're all capable of), but rather repetitive attitudes and behaviors that result in tearing someone down or inhibiting her growth. This behavior is usually accompanied by a lack of awareness, a lack of responsibility, and a lack of change.

Let's look at another example of a relationship that at first might seem disappointing, but when we look at the big picture, we clearly see it is destructive.

The sun shone on Sarah's shoulders—the warmth stoking her hope that today they'd enjoy one another as a family while spending the day at the water park. Jason and Sarah's marriage was on shaky ground, and their three children were feeling the impact. But they'd begun seeing a marriage counselor, and Sarah hoped things might soon change.

There wasn't one big hurt in their relationship like an affair or a beating, but rather an accumulation of many smaller hurts—like when Jason repeatedly took his sister's side in family arguments and sarcastically made fun of Sarah's perspective. Or when Jason continued to allow his parents to enter their home without first calling or knocking, even though Sarah told him how much it bothered her. Or when Jason humiliated her at a family picnic, mocking her and calling her names, and then drove home without her, leaving her stranded. Or when she asked him to trim the bushes and he cut them all down to stubs, even her favorite lilacs. When she protested, he told her they were too much work. Like a thousand bee stings, Jason's offenses over time poisoned Sarah's joy, broke her heart, and crushed her spirit. She grew tired of asking to be heard, hoping to be valued, wanting to be loved.

Floating down the lazy-river ride, all five of them in their own tubes, Sarah turned to Jason and smiled. "I'm so glad we could come here as a family." As she noticed the waterfall ahead, she said, "Uh-oh, I hope I don't get stuck under those falls. I hate that."

Sure enough, Sarah got caught under the falls. For fifteen long seconds, buckets of water pummeled her head as she furiously tried to paddle away. Finally she broke free. Gasping for air, she said, "Sheesh, I can't believe my bad luck."

Jason smiled. They continued floating down the river.

Rounding the corner Sarah saw another waterfall ahead. "Oh no! I do not want to get stuck again."

But for the second time, Sarah's tube lodged directly under the pounding falls. After she escaped, she glared at Jason and asked, "Are *you* doing this?"

"No," he said. "I wouldn't do that to you."

When Sarah's tube stalled under the third waterfall, she put the pieces together. Jason had lodged his big toe under her float and kept her trapped under the falls until he decided to let go. Furious, she jumped out of her tube screaming, "How could you do that to me? I can't believe you lied."

Jason laughed. "Calm down. Don't you think you're overreacting? You get wet at a water park. Can't you have a little fun?"

If Sarah and Jason discussed this incident in a future counseling session, their counselor or pastor might focus on why this bothered Sarah so much. After all, a couple often teases and frolics around with each other. Why was that so offensive to her? Or the counselor might zero in on Jason's immaturity and help him see you don't have fun at another person's expense, even if you're at a water park together. The counselor or pastor might also turn to Sarah and encourage her to let it go, lighten up, or forgive her husband and not hold a grudge. Problem solved—marriage better.

Not true. That approach would be like giving antibiotics to a patient who has lung cancer or an aspirin to someone who is allergic to bee stings. Without a more potent treatment plan, the marriage will die (even if the couple stays legally married).

If we had a wide-angle lens and could look at Jason and Sarah's marriage over the years, we'd see a different picture. The problem with their marriage isn't that Jason is immature and doesn't realize that his playfulness bothers Sarah. Or that Sarah is uptight and overreacts to Jason's attempts to have fun (although both might be true). If we could look over their marital history, we'd see that Jason has consistently been indifferent to what bothers Sarah, and is sometimes intentionally cruel. In spite of what he says, Sarah has no voice or value to him other than being a mother to his children, a maid for the household chores, and a body for sex. He has repeatedly demonstrated that Sarah's feelings, needs, thoughts, or desires don't play a significant part in his decision making. Jason does what Jason wants to do, even when it's at Sarah's expense. That is not playful or merely selfish and immature. When it happens over and over again, despite someone's repeated protests, it is abusive and destructive.

Every marriage has the potential to become destructive because we all are naturally selfish and prideful. Every married couple experiences some frustrations, hurts, unfulfilled expectations, unrealized dreams, and unhappiness throughout their relationship. How we respond to those disappointments can mature us and draw us closer to God and to one another, or we can let those disappointments destroy us and our marriage.

But there are women with marriages like Carol's and Sarah's in every community, in every church. Perhaps you know her. Maybe you are her. Sarah and Carol would be the first to admit they are not perfect wives, but God does not want them to be mocked, sexually humiliated, ignored, verbally battered, lied to, or disrespected. God has a much more glorious answer for these women's lives than "submit and try harder to be a good wife."

How Do You See Your Marriage?

Amy Grant sang a song called "If These Walls Could Speak." If the walls in your home could speak today, what story would they tell about your marriage? How would they describe your friendship with your husband? your sexual relationship? how you handle differences and conflict? how you make up after a fight? your finances? how you make decisions together? your spiritual journey?

When it comes to destructive marriages, it can be quite painful and ugly to see something clearly enough to put it into words. Listen to some of the words other women have used to describe the way they feel in their marriages:

> I can't be his wife and me at the same time. It's either one or the other. In order to stay married to him, I have to stop being me.

> We'd get along fine if I never questioned him and always went along with everything he wanted.

> Every ounce of mental and emotional energy I have is needed to survive living in this marriage. He's so harsh and negative toward everyone and everything I feel like I can't breathe.

> I don't feel safe. His words cut me like a knife. He treats me like I'm his enemy, yet he expects me to want to have sex with him whenever he wants it.

> I don't know how I can keep living like this. The rules never apply to him, only to me.

> Conversations never end. He lectures us and lectures us until we give in and see things his way.

It's always about him, how he feels, what he needs, how he's hurt. There is never any consideration for my feelings, my needs, or my hurts. I exist solely to please him, serve him, and make him happy.

I'm tired of being his mother. He takes no responsibility for anything but constantly blames and criticizes me for everything that goes wrong. Nothing is ever his fault.

I feel like I'm treading water, barely keeping afloat, and he keeps knocking me under. Someday I won't be able to come back up.

I don't know how to live like this anymore. It's either divorce or suicide.

These women did not reach these conclusions after only a single episode of destructive or selfish behavior but after years of repetitive sinful actions and attitudes that their husbands have refused to change. For some women it takes a long time to recognize what's happening, especially if their family of origin contained similar attitudes and behaviors. Maybe you have experienced this.

Other times you can't put what's happening to you into words, but you know something's not right because when you're around your husband, your body feels it. Your stomach churns, your teeth grind, your hands clench, your jaw tightens, your head pounds, your legs shake, and your blood pressure rises. You cry, you can't catch your breath, and you throw up.

Your body is telling you something's wrong. Pay attention.

Sometimes seeing and naming what's wrong can be frightening. I was teaching at a professional counselors' seminar on destructive relationships when one of the participants asked me if she could speak to me privately. During the break we met, and Sherrie shared her story, one that she had never told a single soul before then. While she talked, Sherrie stared at her hands the entire time. When she was finished, she looked up and said, "Just saying it out loud, hearing my own story, I'd say it sounds kind of crazy, doesn't it?"

"Yes, it does," I said.

Before that moment of personal honesty, Sherrie had been telling herself a lie. She was telling herself that things in her marriage weren't that bad. That it was *her* problem. That she was overreacting or being too sensitive to what her husband was doing and saying. But once she spoke aloud what was happening at home, she clearly saw the destruction in her marriage. Once we "see" something, name it, or write it down, it's much harder to deny it to ourselves. Annie Dillard wrote, "Seeing is of course very much a matter of verbalization. Unless I call my attention to what passes before my eyes, I simply won't see it.... I have to say the words, describe what I'm seeing."[1]

I know you understand there is no perfect marriage or perfect husband. The Bible tells us that "we all stumble in many ways" (James 3:2, NIV). Yet, if we want a successful long-term marriage or are going to put the effort into attempting to change an unhappy or destructive one, we must start by naming what we see correctly.

You've picked up this book and read this far for a reason. Remember, Jesus tells us, "If your eye is healthy, your whole body will be full of light" (Matthew 6:22). It's crucial to your well-being as well as to your family's future for you to open your eyes right now in order to see clearly where you are if you want to change where you're going in the future.

Before reading further, I'd like you to take a moment right now and take this quiz. It will help you see if you're in an emotionally destructive marriage.

Are You in an Emotionally Destructive Marriage?

1. My spouse calls me names, such as *stupid* or *worthless,* or uses sexually degrading terms.

   Often   Sometimes   Seldom   Never

2. My spouse mocks and belittles me.

   Often   Sometimes   Seldom   Never

3. My spouse tells me no one else would ever want me as a partner.

   Often   Sometimes   Seldom   Never

4. My spouse pressures me to do things I do not want to do.

   Often   Sometimes   Seldom   Never

5. My spouse threatens to leave me and take the children.

   Often   Sometimes   Seldom   Never

6. My spouse uses the Bible to criticize me or to get me to do something he wants me to do.

   Often   Sometimes   Seldom   Never

7. My spouse tells me who I may have as friends.

   Often   Sometimes   Seldom   Never

8. My spouse dictates how often I can see/talk with my family of origin.

   Often   Sometimes   Seldom   Never

9. My spouse undermines me with our children.

    Often   Sometimes   Seldom   Never

10. My spouse speaks poorly about me to our children.

    Often   Sometimes   Seldom   Never

11. My spouse speaks poorly about me to others (his family, friends, neighbors, church people).

    Often   Sometimes   Seldom   Never

12. I don't feel free to challenge my husband or disagree with him.

    Often   Sometimes   Seldom   Never

13. If I don't agree with my husband or do what he wants, I have a price to pay.

    Often   Sometimes   Seldom   Never

14. My spouse breaks things around the house when he's angry or upset.

    Often   Sometimes   Seldom   Never

15. My spouse screams and curses at me.

    Often   Sometimes   Seldom   Never

16. When I tell my husband my deepest feelings, he laughs at me, ignores me, or uses them against me.

    Often   Sometimes   Seldom   Never

17. My spouse disregards my needs.

    Often   Sometimes   Seldom   Never

18. My spouse tells me I can't live without him.

    Often   Sometimes   Seldom   Never

19. My spouse badgers me until I give in to his demands.

    Often   Sometimes   Seldom   Never

20. My spouse calls or texts me frequently wanting to know where I am, what I am doing, and who I am with.

    Often   Sometimes   Seldom   Never

21. My spouse monitors my e-mails, social-media, and Internet use.

    Often   Sometimes   Seldom   Never

22. My spouse accuses me of things I did not do.

    Often   Sometimes   Seldom   Never

23. My spouse demands my attention when I'm busy with something or someone else.

    Often   Sometimes   Seldom   Never

24. My spouse does not like it when I get positive attention or affirmation from other people—friends, family, church, work.

    Often   Sometimes   Seldom   Never

25. My spouse tells me I cannot tell anyone what happens between us.

    Often   Sometimes   Seldom   Never

26. My spouse uses sarcasm and ridicule to get me to stop talking or to change my mind about something.

    Often   Sometimes   Seldom   Never

27. My spouse refuses to listen to my point of view.

    Often   Sometimes   Seldom   Never

28. My spouse blows up when I ask questions about why he did something.

    Often   Sometimes   Seldom   Never

29. My spouse physically restrains me to keep me from leaving a volatile situation.

    Often   Sometimes   Seldom   Never

30. My spouse has threatened to harm me.

    Often   Sometimes   Seldom   Never

31. My spouse uses physical force to get me to do something he wants me to do or to stop doing something he doesn't want me to do.

    Often   Sometimes   Seldom   Never

32. My spouse has injured me.

    Often   Sometimes   Seldom   Never

33. My spouse threatens to harm things that are important to me (children, pets, reputation, and property).

    Often   Sometimes   Seldom   Never

34. My spouse uses physical force to coerce me sexually.

    Often   Sometimes   Seldom   Never

35. My spouse withdraws from me if I don't do what he wants.

    Often   Sometimes   Seldom   Never

36. My spouse refuses to respond when I ask him questions.

    Often   Sometimes   Seldom   Never

37. My spouse changes the subject when I try to bring up something that's bothering me.

    Often   Sometimes   Seldom   Never

38. My spouse ignores me for long periods of time.

    Often   Sometimes   Seldom   Never

39. My spouse refuses to engage or participate in everyday family life.

    Often   Sometimes   Seldom   Never

40. My spouse plays mind games with me.

    Often   Sometimes   Seldom   Never

41. My spouse tells me that he's the one who is being mistreated by me.

    Often   Sometimes   Seldom   Never

42. My spouse says the problems in our marriage are all my fault.

    Often   Sometimes   Seldom   Never

43. My spouse acts one way in public and another way at home.

    Often   Sometimes   Seldom   Never

44. There is a double standard around what's acceptable behavior. He gives himself more leeway than he gives me.

    Often   Sometimes   Seldom   Never

45. My spouse refuses to tell me how much money he earns.

    Often   Sometimes   Seldom   Never

46. I have no voice regarding how our finances are saved or spent.

    Often   Sometimes   Seldom   Never

47. I have no idea what my husband does with our money even though I've asked.

    Often   Sometimes   Seldom   Never

48. My spouse tells me things that I know are not true.

    Often   Sometimes   Seldom   Never

49. My spouse omits information that keeps me from knowing the whole story about something.

    Often   Sometimes   Seldom   Never

50. My spouse lies to other people (children, work colleagues, friends, church, family, IRS, police, etc.).

    Often   Sometimes   Seldom   Never

51. I feel crazy in my marriage.

    Often   Sometimes   Seldom   Never

52. I feel trapped in my marriage.

    Often   Sometimes   Seldom   Never

53. I don't feel I can be myself in my marriage.

    Often   Sometimes   Seldom   Never

54. I feel like a child in my marriage.

    Often   Sometimes   Seldom   Never

55. I feel like his mother in my marriage.

    Often   Sometimes   Seldom   Never

56. I feel tense around my spouse.

    Often   Sometimes   Seldom   Never

57. I feel angry around my spouse.

    Often   Sometimes   Seldom   Never

58. I feel afraid of my spouse.

    Often   Sometimes   Seldom   Never

59. My children are afraid of my spouse.

    Often   Sometimes   Seldom   Never

60. I feel physically ill around my spouse.

    Often   Sometimes   Seldom   Never

61. I am using medications, excess food, and/or alcohol to cope
    with my marriage.

    Often   Sometimes   Seldom   Never

If you answered the last eleven questions (51–61) with *Often* and *Sometimes,* your marriage is taking a toll on you and it's important that you not ignore what's happening to you.

Go back through your answers to questions 1–50 and see how many questions you answered with *Often* and *Sometimes.* What do you see? What's the pattern, the big picture? If you answered more than two questions with *Often,* your marriage may become or is becoming destructive. If you answered *Often* for more than five questions, it is definitely destructive. If you answered *Sometimes* and *Seldom* for some or many of the questions but did not circle *Often,* your marriage is or is becoming destructive. Please take action now before things get worse. In chapter 3 I will go into more detail about the different types of destructive relationships and why they are destructive. Here is a breakdown of what the questions look for.

Questions 1–28 describe the various characteristics in an emotionally abusive relationship. Belittling, humiliating, badgering, controlling, undermining, and threatening are obvious characteristics of emotional abuse.

Questions 20–24 indicate jealousy and inappropriate dependency, which lead to being destructive.

Questions 28–34 describe physically abusive tactics used to express displeasure or to force someone to do something she does not want to do. Threats to harm are considered abusive. This is controlling abuse.

Questions 35–39 look for more covert indicators of emotional abuse. They aren't as obvious as some of the other tactics used to control, but they are effective. They also indicate gross indifference to the feelings and needs of the spouse, which is destructive to a marriage.

Questions 40–44 describe the vague area of crazy-making where you can't define what is abusive, but the mind games, the refusal to engage, and the blaming leave you confused and uncertain.

Questions 45–47 describe coercive control with respect to the family finances.

Questions 48–50 describe deceit, which breaks trust and destroys the very foundation of marriage.

Questions 51–61 look for your responses to what's happening in your marriage. Some individuals may be more resilient to some of these destructive behaviors, others not. Don't compare yourself with anyone else who may be able to live with something when your body and your spirit are breaking down.

In summary, an emotionally destructive marriage is one where one's personhood, dignity, and freedom of choice is regularly denied, criticized, or crushed. This can be done through words, behaviors, economics, attitudes, and misusing the Scriptures.

An emotionally destructive marriage is one where one's personhood, dignity, and freedom of choice is regularly denied, criticized, or crushed. This can be done through words, behaviors, economics, attitudes, and misusing the Scriptures.

Taking the quiz and answering the questions was tough, but it also may have provided a bit of relief to see more clearly what's going on. If you've ever been lost in a bad place and have no idea where you are, it's a terrifying feeling. If you want to find your way out, you start by seeing where you are right now. Believe me. No one wants to be in a destructive marriage. But hope for change is birthed when you can see clearly where you are and where you need to go. Only when you do that can you take the first step.

Don't despair. I'm going to give you a map to follow. With God's help, you will find your way through.

Dear God,

Sometimes I'm afraid to open my eyes and see what's going on in my home. I don't want to know. It scares me. But I want to trust you with my life, my children, and my marriage. I want to believe that you see what's going on and you want it to stop. I want to know your wisdom and your ways so that I am not destroyed by the pain I'm in. Help me, God, take one step at a time.

Action Step: Buy yourself a journal and begin to process what you see about your marriage from reading this chapter and taking the test. Be as honest with yourself as you know how. This is essential if you want to know where you are. If you are worried that your husband might read your journal, you can write in a password-protected file on your computer. If you answered *Often* on many of the questions, it's important that you start to document what's going on for your own protection. Please read about how to do that in chapter 8.

Two

The Three Essential Ingredients in a Thriving Relationship

They do not fear bad news;
>   they confidently trust the Lord to care for them.

—Psalm 112:7, NLT

Many of us have grown up in homes where sinful attitudes and destructive behavior are accepted as normal. We're so used to being mistreated or disrespected, controlled or manipulated that we don't recognize it as such.

During a counseling session, one of my clients asked me how often my husband cursed me out. When I told her he never did, she didn't believe me. All the men she knew, Christian or otherwise, regularly cursed at their wives and children when they got mad. Some of you have had similar experiences.

On the other hand, some of you grew up on a steady diet observing Hollywood's and Harlequin's version of love and marriage. They portray unrealistic and distorted ideas around love and marriage. They want you to believe that if you have enough sexual passion, the rest of the relationship is easy.

And finally, others of you grew up in stable, loving families, but your own marriage is nothing like that. You fear your children won't have the same sense of security and love you grew up with, but you don't know what to do to change it.

Let's look at the basic ingredients necessary for a relationship to be healthy and why these basics are crucial for a marriage to flourish.

ESSENTIALS TO THRIVING RELATIONSHIPS

Every grown-up relationship requires three essential ingredients to thrive: mutuality, reciprocity, and freedom.

Mutuality means that both individuals contribute specific qualities essential for the care, maintenance, and repair of the relationship. These qualities are honesty, caring, respect, responsibility, and repentance. In marriage, both individuals make efforts to grow and change for the welfare of the other and the preservation of their relationship.[1]

Destructive relationships lack mutuality. One of my clients, Sally, was concerned about her daughter, Marie, who was about to get married. Sally divorced Marie's father when Marie was five because of his irresponsibility and chronic adultery. Sally feared that Marie did not have a good role model for a responsible man for marriage. When Marie got engaged, her mother begged her to speak with me first, just to make sure her relationship with Ed was healthy. Marie reluctantly agreed to one session.

"Marie, tell me what you like best about your relationship with Ed," I said.

"Oh, he's wonderful," she said, smiling. "He's smart and funny, and we have so much fun. I've never met anyone who can make me laugh like Ed can."

As we talked back and forth, I sensed that Marie deeply loved Ed. She saw his strengths, but she also saw at least one of his weaknesses. She said, "I know he's a little too lazy at times. Mom's worried that he won't be a good provider. But I think he needs encouragement. He'll come along."

"Are there other ways that you notice Ed is lazy?"

"Well, I wouldn't call it lazy. He says he's easier going than I am. Things don't bother him like they do me. Sometimes his bills are a little late or he bounces checks. Or he forgets to do what he said he'd do for me."

"What happens when you try to talk to him or tell him that it bothers you?"

"He tells me I'm overreacting, and I probably am. I think I'm wound too tight. I need a man like Ed to help me have more fun in my life."

"I certainly can understand that you need to have fun in your life. But it also sounds like you value being a responsible person. Is that right?"

Marie nodded.

After getting more details about their relationship and Ed's lack of responsibility, I said to Marie, "It doesn't sound like there is much mutual responsibility in this relationship, Marie. You seem to be doing most of the work to maintain the connection, financially support your lives together, and bail Ed out of messes. Do you think that will get old after a while?"

Marie thought about it for a minute and said, "I think he'll change. He just needs to grow up a little more."

"And if he doesn't, then what?"

Marie did not want to look at that possibility. But those of you who are married to men who haven't matured want to grab her by the shoulders and shake her awake and shout, "Don't do it! He'll never change as long as you're the mom."

Tim Keller, in his book on marriage, wrote, "The Christian teaching [on marriage] does not offer a choice between fulfillment and sacrifice but rather mutual fulfillment through mutual sacrifice."[2] When you are the only one in your marriage caring, repenting, being respectful and honest, sacrificing, and working toward being a better spouse, you are a godly wife, but you don't have a healthy or biblical marriage.

> When you are the only one in your marriage caring, repenting, being respectful and honest, sacrificing, and working toward being a better spouse, you are a godly wife, but you don't have a healthy or biblical marriage.

Paul wrote about the importance of mutuality in healthy relationships throughout his teachings. For example, he wrote, "We have spoken freely to you, Corinthians, and opened wide our hearts to you. We are not withholding our affection from you, but you are withholding yours from us. As a fair exchange—I speak as to my children—open wide your hearts also" (2 Corinthians 6:11–13, NIV).

Paul also emphasized mutuality throughout his teaching on marriage. Husbands and wives may have different roles and responsibilities, but he calls both to mutually fulfill them. Paul explained the mutuality of the sexual relationship. He wrote, "The husband should give to his wife her conjugal rights, and *likewise* the wife to her husband. For the wife does not have authority over her own body, but the husband does. *Likewise* the husband does not have authority over his own body, but the wife does" (1 Corinthians 7:3–4).

Peter, too, spoke of mutuality when he wrote, "*Likewise*, wives, be subject to your own husbands, so that even if some do not obey the word, they may be won without a word by the conduct of their wives, when they see your respectful and pure conduct.… *Likewise*, husbands, live with your wives in an understanding way, showing honor to the woman as the weaker vessel, since they are heirs with you of the grace of life, so that your prayers may not be hindered" (1 Peter 3:1–2, 7).

These instructions to husbands and wives work great *only* when they are practiced by both the husband and the wife. Both are to give and both are to sacrifice to meet the needs of the other. When these directives are not practiced mutually, it is a very different picture. That does not give you permission to give up or to disobey God's instructions, although that path is tempting when you feel mistreated and angry. Instead, talk to God about how to handle this lack of mutuality and your hurt feelings. You do not have the power to turn a bad marriage into a good marriage all by yourself. But Peter reminds us that by our godly attitude and actions, we can behave in ways that can influence our husbands to surrender to God's transforming work of change in their lives (see 1 Peter 3). Throughout this book I'll show you wise ways you can do this, even when your marriage is destructive.

This brings us to the second essential ingredient of a thriving relationship: reciprocity.

Reciprocity means that both people in the relationship give and both people in the relationship receive. Power and responsibility are shared. There is not a double standard where one person gets all the goodies in the relationship while the other person sacrificially does most of the work. The apostle Paul validates reciprocity with guidelines on how to give our resources sacrificially but not foolishly. He wrote, "For I do not mean that others should be eased and you burdened, but that as a matter of fairness your abundance at the present time should supply their need, so that their abundance may supply your need, that there may be fairness" (2 Corinthians 8:13–14).

Destructive marriages are not reciprocal and therefore don't thrive. One person demands power over the other and relegates his or her partner to the status of a slave or a child. For example, John required Mary to be accountable for every penny she spent, yet John did not hold himself to that same standard. He always had an excuse as to why his spending was more justified than Mary's and often spent large amounts of money without telling her. Mary worked a full-time job, as did John. Mary was required to direct deposit her entire paycheck into their joint account. John only deposited an equal dollar amount of his paycheck into their joint account. The rest of his income was put in a separate account with only his name on it. Mary had no access to it, nor did she even know what John's income was. There was no "we" to their financial decisions; John held all the financial power. Mary felt like a child being given an allowance. To rebalance their marriage and create a healthier relationship, Mary will need to speak up and require more reciprocity from John. And John will have to change how he sees and treats Mary. She needs to become his partner, not his possession, if their marriage is to become healthy. (How to have that kind of discussion will be covered in section 3.)

Something to keep in mind is that there may be seasons in every marriage where one person gives more than the other, due to illness, incapacity, or other problems; but when that happens, as soon as the individual is capable, the relationship is rebalanced and power and responsibility are again mutually shared.

Lastly, our third essential ingredient of a thriving relationship is freedom.

Freedom means that in your marriage you are allowed to make choices, give input, and express your feelings without fearing you'll be badgered, manipulated, and punished. When freedom is present, you're not afraid to be yourself nor are you pressured to become something you're not.

Freedom is an essential component in all healthy adult relationships. We've all witnessed the results in world history, in fundamentalist religious groups, and in families where freedom is squashed. Members are not free to question, to challenge, to think differently from the group. They are not free to grow or be themselves without fear of retaliation.

Instead, they have to do and say and be what the group or person in charge tells them. That is not healthy, nor is it God's plan. Although God wants unity in a family and in the family of God, he created great diversity. We are to be ourselves and be of one mind all at the same time. This one-mind idea doesn't mean melding ourselves into the desires or demands of another individual, but together living for a common purpose and goal—the kingdom and glory of God.

Married couples need freedom to thrive. I do not mean the freedom to do whatever you want regardless how the other person feels. When you commit to someone in marriage, you freely choose to limit some (not all) of your choices. But all healthy relationships need to include freedom for the individuals to disagree, to respectfully challenge the other's decisions, and to be the persons God made them to be. Having your freedom of movement, choices, friends, and emotional expression restricted by your husband sends the message that you are not allowed to be a whole person in your own marriage. Instead, you are to become what your husband tells you to be.

At a retreat where I was recently speaking, a young woman approached me during a break. Aimee said, "My husband doesn't like the way I dress, but I don't know how to respond to that. I like the clothes I wear. What should I do?"

"What doesn't he like about the way you dress?" I asked.

"He says men look at me. He wants me to wear baggier jeans, long dresses, and no makeup."

"What do you think about that?" I asked, concerned that she was feeling pressured to become someone else in order to pacify her husband's insecurity.

"I think I dress modestly. I don't seek out attention, but I don't want to be frumpy either. But he said if I loved him, I would dress to please him, not myself."

Immediately I felt great concern for this woman's dilemma. Her husband twisted the Scripture and put himself in God's place in her life. The Bible says we are to please God, not ourselves. Nor are we to orient our lives around pleasing others; that gets us in trouble (see Galatians 1:10, 1 Thessalonians 2:4). That does not mean we are to have no thoughts of pleasing our husbands, but pleasing our husbands is not to be our first concern. And it's important to understand that pleasing God by pleasing our husbands does not always work. Sometimes we will please God and displease our husbands, like when we stand up for what is right, true, and good and our husbands get mad or feel threatened.

Here is what I told Aimee: "You need to be very wise right now as you're at a critical crossroads in your marriage. If you give in to him in this, you will lose a part of who you are to satisfy a part of him that is sinful and immature—his insecurity. That is not healthy for either of you or for the long-term stability of your marriage. It's up to you, but I think God calls you to be courageous in this moment and lovingly tell your husband you think he needs to face his own issues of jealousy and insecurity, rather than you changing your wardrobe so that he won't feel those feelings. He will not like it at first, but in the long run, this approach will preserve your freedom to be your own person and to speak truthfully into his life, which is essential for a healthy marriage."

A GENTLE WARNING

Some of you are trembling right now because you are becoming more aware of the high cost you have paid to cater to your husband's demands. You see that your marriage lacks mutuality, reciprocity, and freedom. You've given in again and again because you believed that was the right thing to do, but it's taken its toll on you. You've become weak and fragile, fearful and depressed—a shell of your former self. Your marriage has not gotten healthier or happier as a result of all your efforts to please. The thought of making even the smallest change right now feels too hard, the price too high. You're terrified that if you rock your marital boat ever so slightly, you and your children will tumble out into the sea and drown.

I do want to warn you. When you stop pretending and try to make some changes, there is always the possibility that your spouse will react negatively. He may see it as you vying for power and may attempt to flatten you back down by his strong negative reaction. I know it feels too big, too overwhelming, to even think of making changes. But there is something inside of you that knows you must—not only for you, but for your children and even for your marriage. Throughout this book I will help you gain strength and courage, as well as teach you the steps you need to take. You can learn to stand up and stand strong in who you are in Christ, so that you will become a healthy and godly woman.

> ### Dear God,
> *I am scared. I see how important mutuality, reciprocity, and freedom are to having a healthy marriage. I want that too, but I have no idea how to make it happen. Please give me wisdom and courage not to turn back or continue to pretend everything is fine when it's not.*

Action Step: Below are sixteen traits of a healthy marriage. Answer the questions to see whether your marriage is relatively healthy, even if it is disappointing.

1. My spouse shows care and concern for me and my needs.
   Yes No
2. My spouse has my best interests in mind. **Yes No**

3. My spouse asks my opinion on things. **Yes No**

4. My spouse trusts me. **Yes No**

5. My spouse works with me as a partner to parent our children.
   Yes No

6. My spouse is willing to get help for our marriage problems.
   Yes No

7. My spouse takes responsibility and apologizes when he's wrong.
   Yes No

8. My spouse asks for my opinion on things in our marriage.
   Yes No

9. My spouse is considerate of my feelings. **Yes No**

10. When we have a problem, my spouse is willing to talk about it.
    Yes No

11. My spouse uses the Bible to correct his own life. **Yes No**

12. My spouse listens to advice from wise people. **Yes No**

13. My spouse allows me to be myself. **Yes No**

14. My spouse allows me to make my own decisions. **Yes No**

15. My spouse allows me to disagree. **Yes No**

16. My spouse is a good steward with our finances. **Yes No**

If you answered yes to most of these questions, your marriage is relatively healthy. One or two nos indicate some weak areas in your marriage. More than three nos indicate an unhealthy marriage. More than five nos indicate a destructive marriage.

Three

Five Patterns That Destroy a Relationship and Damage People

Their insults have broken my heart,
and I am in despair.

—Psalm 69:20, NLT

God designed marriage to be a lifelong, loving partnership. Marriage and family life is intended to be a safe place and should not feel like a war zone or a concentration camp. Marriage not only provides loving companionship and a committed bond to raise children, but it helps us mature and put into practice the lessons of sacrifice and servanthood. Successful family life requires that we love when we don't feel like it, resolve conflict when there are differences and disagreements, and care about the needs of others as much as we care about our own. These actions and attitudes don't come naturally. They must be learned.

No marriage reaches these ideals all the time. That is why most of you who took the quizzes in chapters 1 and 2 may have found some areas that need attention. You may be working hard to make it better, or you may be making it worse by the way you're handling your disappointment.

In this chapter, we'll look at five different types of behaviors and attitudes that cause marriages to fail precisely because they are destructive and wound people. These five patterns—reactive abuse, controlling abuse, deceit, dependence, and indifference—may appear in varying combinations, intensities, and degrees in destructive marriages. But even if you identify with only one of these five, when repeatedly practiced with no repentance or change, a healthy and godly marriage is impossible, even if you choose to stay legally married.

REACTIVE ABUSE

Reactive abuse occurs when a husband or wife or both are unable to manage their negative moods, the frustrations of life, or their tempers in a mature way. As a result, when situations are provocative or there is stress, an eruption occurs. In reactive abuse, a person doesn't stop to think about the wisest way to handle a difficult or irritating situation; he or she just reacts. We criticize, curse, yell, threaten, throw things, belittle, punch, slap, and even murder. The Bible warns us, "In your anger do not sin" (Ephesians 4:26, NIV).

In an all-too-common marital exchange, Donna felt crabby and overwhelmed. The kids were screaming, and there were dirty dishes and toys all over the house. Instead of asking for help, she started yelling at her husband who was relaxing, watching the news after a hard day's work.

"Why can't you ever lift a finger to help around here? Can't you see I'm struggling? What's wrong with you?"

Ben rolled his eyes. "Shut up and quit nagging. I work hard. What do you do all day besides sit around and play on the computer?"

"How dare you!" Donna said, as she flung one of the children's plastic toys at Ben, hitting him in the back of his head. "You have no idea how hard I work taking care of these kids and this house. You're such a loser."

"Me!" Ben said, jumping up from the couch, whipping the toy right back at Donna. "What about you? I was just relaxing, minding my own business when you started it."

Furious and hurt, Donna and Ben spent the rest of the evening in stony silence, neither one willing to wave the white flag or apologize. The apostle Paul warns us, "If you keep on biting and devouring each other, watch out or you will be destroyed by each other" (Galatians 5:15, NIV). Disappointment and frustration occur every day and in every relationship. We don't always cope well with our normal frustrations or tolerate our own negative emotions or communicate them maturely. When that happens, sinful and abusive reactions are much more likely.[1]

For instance, Ellie caught her husband looking at pornography, and in her pain and fury, she picked up his hammer and smashed his computer to pieces (as well as a few other things he valued).

In another example, Tom was cut off by a reckless driver who swerved in front of him. In his rage, Tom drove like a maniac, terrifying his wife and kids who feared for their safety.

Later, after they've calmed down, they rarely apologize or take responsibility for scaring their family or losing control of themselves. If someone confronts them on their abusive actions and attitudes, they often point the finger.

For example, Tom said, "If the driver didn't cut me off, this wouldn't have happened."

Ellie said, "If you weren't watching disgusting porn, your computer would still be here."

Donna said, "If Ben would just help me more…"

Ben said, "If only she would have asked me nicely…"

Ever since Adam blamed Eve for giving him the forbidden fruit, we all shift blame. Can you hear yourself? You're held captive by your own storyline that says you had no choice but to respond the way you did. You tell yourself the only reason you reacted that way is because of the other person's wrong. Therefore, your response is their fault. The deceptive part of this thinking is that there is a smidgen of truth in it. Imagine what a wonderful person you could be if your husband, children, mother, friend, or neighbor did exactly what you wanted them to do when you wanted them to do it, all the time. Imagine how kind you would be if people never upset you, never disappointed you, or never hurt your feelings. Imagine how loving you would be if life went exactly the way you wanted it to. The problem with this thinking is that it's pure fantasy. People do provoke us. They let us down. We get disappointed and frustrated. Others don't always love us as we'd like them to or do exactly what we want. Our wrong and hurtful reactions to life's frustrations and disappointments are understandable, but they usually make things worse.

Reactive abuse in a marriage can be something just one person regularly does or the couple can feed off of each other, reacting abusively back and forth. Either way, when reactive abuse is part of a marriage, it is destructive, not only to the marriage, but also to their children who often become the casualties of the war at home.

In addition, it can be difficult for pastors, people helpers, and even trained counselors to tell the difference between reactive abuse and our next destructive pattern, controlling abuse. The abusive behaviors look similar, but the underlying heart issues are not. An important distinction is that in reactive abuse the destructive person is not seeking to control his wife or to broadly exercise decision-making power over her. That does not minimize the lethality of reactive abuse. When we become flooded with negative emotions and don't know how to control ourselves, we can cause a lot of harm.

Controlling Abuse

Throughout marriage a healthy couple negotiates, compromises, sacrifices, and mutually submits for the welfare of their relationship and the love of each other. Threats and force should never be used to make the other give in. When that happens, it is controlling abuse and it's destructive.

Teresa knew Bill's rules. One of them was she was not allowed to talk on the phone when he was home. He reasoned that she had all day to talk to her family and friends, if she wanted to. Shortly after dinner Teresa's sister called. She needed some advice on a problem with her computer and wanted Teresa's help. Teresa felt torn. She wanted to help her sister, but she knew if she talked with her right now, she'd have a price to pay later.

"Bill," Teresa whispered, holding her hand over the phone, "Denise needs my help with something on her computer. I'll just be a few minutes."

Bill cocked his brow, glaring at Teresa.

When she got off the phone, Bill was fuming. "Once again I see I come last in your life," he said.

"That's not true," Teresa protested. "But I wanted to help Denise. She had an important work project and needed to use her computer tonight."

Bill grabbed for Teresa's phone and hurled it in the sink, full of soapy water. "Now I guess you won't be able to talk on the phone when I'm home."

Controlling abuse may look similar to reactive abuse, but the roots are very different. Bill did react abusively to Teresa's decision to help her sister, but what makes this controlling abuse is that Bill believes Teresa has no right to make an independent decision if he disagrees. If confronted with his behavior, Bill will say, "I've told Teresa I don't like her talking on the phone when I'm home. It's her fault I got so mad." In Bill's mind, the core problem is with Teresa. He thinks she was at fault for putting her sister's needs ahead of him and his needs, and that she is not loving him or submitting to his headship.

The issue of submission is a crossroads where Christians often get muddled. Does Bill have the right as her husband to dictate Teresa's phone use? Let's broaden it further. Does a husband have the right to control how his wife spends her free time, what she wears, the friends she chooses, how much time she spends with her family, what she buys, how she thinks, what she feels, the things she needs to work on or change, and ultimately who she should be? Is biblical headship synonymous with taking control over someone else and forcing her to comply when she resists? And, does biblical submission require a wife to always do what her husband says? Does it mean she has no choices of her own or can't ever say no without being labeled as rebellious or ungodly?

Remember, a healthy adult relationship includes the freedom to be you, to have your own individuality and personality, and to make choices. Bill certainly has the freedom to express his preferences and his feelings about wanting to spend time with Teresa without interruption, and even to ask her to limit her phone time while he is home. But Teresa (as an adult woman) must also have the freedom to choose to help her sister, express her own feelings, and be herself without fear of punishment or retribution from her husband. Even if Bill was disappointed in Teresa's choices, she has the right to make them. In a healthy marriage, when a couple faces a conflict of values or priorities, they talk it through, respecting each other's perspective. (If you'd like to know how a healthy couple manages such disagreements, go to www.leslievernick.com/the -emotionally-destructive-marriage and look for "Bill and Teresa's Argument: How They Resolve It in a Godly Way.")

Counselors sometimes confuse controlling abuse with reactive abuse. Hopefully, they would identify Bill's actions as sinful, but what often happens next is that the counselor turns to the wife and encourages her to stop pushing her husband's buttons. This is a grave counseling error but especially troublesome in cases of controlling abuse. This implies it's the wife's responsibility to anticipate and manage her husband's emotions. It also feeds his craving for unlimited control and endorses his mistaken belief that he gets to make the rules for her to live by.

Controlling abuse can take many forms and can be mild to life threatening. A husband can use his physical strength to force his wife to do something she doesn't want to do, like Bill did with Teresa. He can also use verbal threats, harsh and demeaning words, finances, and even the Scriptures to overpower her. When someone is vying for total control over someone, physical force is never sufficient. In *Getting Free,* author Ginny Nicarthy comments about a report on torture from Amnesty International,

> Most people who brainwash…use methods similar to those of prison guards, who recognize that physical control is never easily accomplished without the cooperation of the prisoner. The most effective way to gain that cooperation is through subversive manipulation of the mind and feelings of the victim, who then becomes a psychological, as well as a physical, prisoner.[2]

In other words, if you want control over someone, play mind games with her. Add emotional manipulation. Create confusion of what's real and what's true. Isolate her from others. Keep her up late, don't let her sleep, badger her until she gives in. Threaten to hurt her, her children, her pets, her possessions, her reputation. Tell her God is on your side. Degrade her, humiliate her, and enforce trivial demands. Refuse responsibility and instead blame, accuse, and attack. Control the money so she has no resources and is completely dependent on you for everything. And keep her ambivalent about leaving the marriage by periodically performing small acts of kindness. Bring home her favorite flowers, clean up the kitchen, or allow her to go out with her girlfriends. That will keep her grateful for your gestures, and she will try to make things better. It stokes her hope (fantasy) that someday things will be different.

These tactics to gain control over others are used by the military on prisoners of war and are so effective that religious cults use them to keep their members compliant.[3] They should never be used in a marriage. They work at systematically destroying the personhood of the other, leaving her in a diminished capacity to resist, to break free, or to think clearly on her own.

When a woman starts to wake up from her dream of a loving marriage and realizes that she's trapped in a nightmare, she feels desperate. She often slides into a dark depression. But sooner or later, little by little, she must start to fight and claw her way free from her husband's oppressive control if she is going to survive. She now understands she's been captured, muzzled, restricted like a child, or buried alive, and she must fight for her physical, emotional, mental, and spiritual health.

Once a woman starts to fight back, her rage and hurt often get expressed in sinful and destructive ways. She may appear irrational, ungodly, unstable, controlling, mean, and even a little crazy to those who don't know the whole story of what she's been through and what she lives with.

DECEIT

Kim always told everyone she had a great marriage. She and Dave had been together for over thirty years, married right out of high school. They raised three beautiful girls and were looking forward to an empty nest and enjoying this next season of their life together. Then the bottom fell out.

"Leslie, I can't believe I was so naive," Kim said, as she wrapped her arms tightly around her bony torso while her body visibly shook. "I trusted my husband. I thought we had a secure relationship. Never in a million years would I have believed this would happen."

Dave slouched in my other chair, clearly uncomfortable sitting in a counselor's office. When I turned to him, he shrugged. "It meant nothing to me. I told Kim that. It's over. I'm sorry. I was wrong. I made a mistake."

"I love my husband," Kim continued. "I want my marriage. But I don't know how to fix this. He's always told me that I was everything he ever wanted. Even throughout these past two years, he told me that. What does that mean now? I don't believe anything he says anymore." Kim held her head in her hands. "I'm so messed up. I have no idea who my husband is."

As I began to talk with both of them, their great marriage began to reveal a lot of holes. Dave was handsome, charming, and charismatic, but he was also wily and immature. He wasn't able or willing to look at himself or his reasons for his long-term deceit or betrayal. He chalked it up to falling into temptation.

"Leslie," he said, throwing his hands into the air, "I'm no different than a million other guys. When a woman throws herself at you, it's hard to resist. What can I say?"

Dave was in my office to patch things up and get back to normal as quickly as possible, but Kim realized that there was no normal to return to. Seeing her husband's deceit over the past two years, his callous sexual relationships with other women, and his current indifference to her own suffering opened Kim's eyes to other areas in their relationship that she had long overlooked.

"I'm seeing things now I've never seen before and I'm terrified. I can't close my eyes and not see them anymore, but I have no idea where to go from here. I feel like I'm losing my mind," Kim said.

Dave folded his arms and sighed, frustrated with Kim's emotional volatility and the counseling process. He hoped a Christian counselor would tell Kim she needed to forgive him and let it go. He said he was sorry. He promised he wouldn't do it again. Case closed—all better. For Kim, it wasn't that simple.

Anyone who is honest wouldn't be able to claim that he or she never lies. We all do it, because lying is part of our sin nature. For example, we tell our friend we're busy and we can't get together, when the truth is that we want the day to ourselves or that she gets on our nerves. We're running late for a meeting, but instead of confessing that we didn't manage our time well, we tell our boss we got caught in traffic. We call our credit card company claiming we never received the bill, yet we know we're so disorganized with our mail, it's probably there somewhere and we just can't find it. We excuse and rationalize these little lies because we don't see their harm.

We lie when we withhold information that, if known by the other person, would cause conflict, challenge, or consequence. We also lie when we deliberately make up excuses or stories or give someone information that misleads, confuses, deceives, or hurts another person. The more we do this, the more destructive it becomes in our relationships because it breaks trust. When we don't tell the truth in little things where the conflict, challenge, or consequences would be minor, why would our spouse trust us to tell the truth in big things?

Jack often lied to his wife when she followed up with him on something she asked him to do. He lied because it was easier to tell her he did it than to face Jennifer's disappointment and frustration with him for not doing it. For example, when she asked him if he'd finished filling out the taxes, Jack told her he had, when the truth was he meant to, but just hadn't gotten around to it yet. Jack often procrastinated and didn't do the things he said he would. This drove Jennifer crazy, especially when Jack intentionally misled Jennifer into thinking things were taken care of.

During a counseling session, Jennifer said, "If he'd told me that he hadn't done the taxes yet, I wouldn't have liked it, but at least I would have known where it stood. This way, I'm blindsided when we get the late notice and I find out Jack lied about it. And, now we have a penalty to pay." Jennifer's disappointment and anger with Jack, however, did not motivate him to look at himself, acknowledge his weaknesses, or work to be more responsible. Instead, when she confronted him, he became defensive and blamed her.

"I never do anything good enough for you, do I?" Jack screamed. "You're something else. I don't know another guy who would put up with all your nagging!"

Jack's outburst was a defensive maneuver meant to divert attention from his own feelings of shame and inadequacy. Instead of looking at himself, he accused Jennifer of being critical and having unrealistic expectations. When Jack does this, Jennifer becomes the problem rather than his own procrastination, lying, and irresponsibility. She is overreacting or making a big deal out of nothing. She is unreasonable and no man would put up with her. Jack not only lies to Jennifer, but he also lies to himself. He now sees himself as the victim of Jennifer's nagging or overreaction, all the while refusing to take a good hard look at himself.

Once deceit is discovered, there are often a lot of diversionary tactics to avoid taking full responsibility, not only for the sin of lying but for the damage it's caused the spouse and the marriage. For example, during a counseling session with Dave and Kim, Kim was still trying to process the hurt around his deceit and unfaithfulness, and Dave got angry.

"The past is the past," Dave said. "I told you I'm sorry. Why can't you wipe the slate clean and start over?" Dave sees the problem as Kim's lack of grace and continued resentment.

Please don't misunderstand. Dave may have some valid points in addressing Kim's continued resentment and lack of grace as being obstacles to their eventual reconciliation. But Dave, too, must be willing to look at his pattern of deceit, as well as the pain he's caused his wife, if their marriage is truly going to recover from his infidelity and rebuild trust as its foundation.

When deceit and attack become a regular part of marital interactions, there is no clear communication, no resolution to the problem, and no healing. It's impossible to have a close, loving relationship with someone you can't trust, can't talk with, or who won't take a look at himself when he hurts you. Couples can sweep things under the rug only so long before one or the other starts tripping over the huge lump in the room.

> It's impossible to have a close, loving relationship with someone you can't trust, can't talk with, or who won't take a look at himself when he hurts you.

Lying can also be intentionally cruel and malicious. During their separation, Sam told the pastor that his wife, Jane, was bipolar and suffering from borderline personality disorder. Sam had come to these conclusions by doing some research over the Internet, but his wife had never seen a mental-health professional or received such a diagnosis. However, the pastor assumed Sam knew what he was talking about and was telling the truth. Sam's deceit negatively influenced the pastor's view of Jane and all she subsequently shared with him. Sam played that card to his advantage during their separation.

When we make up stories or give false reports or even half truths about our spouses and share these with in-laws, parents, friends, neighbors, church leaders, and counselors, our goal is to destroy the dignity, reputation, and personhood of our spouses. God hates lying and warns us that sometimes it is those closest to us who become our greatest enemies (see Psalm 55:20–21; Proverbs 6:16–17; Micah 7:1–6; Obadiah 1:7).

Controlling abuse and deceit often work together. If you want control over someone, lying and manipulating information is one way to confuse her and control her perceptions (or other people's perceptions) on what's real and what's true. Marriage is anchored on trust, and it is impossible to have a successful long-term relationship with someone you don't trust, even if you love him. Once trust is broken, it is not easily repaired. It takes a consistent effort from the one who broke the trust to earn it back, as well as a willingness to forgive by the one betrayed.

Dependence

God created human beings to live in dependence on him. When the Lord instructed Adam and Eve not to eat the forbidden fruit, he wanted them to completely rely on him for all things good. Sadly, they chose to go outside the boundaries God established. They rejected the God-ordained limits of their humanness and believed the lie that they could be as God (see Genesis 3:5). As a consequence of their disobedience, we all have the same bent. We strive to be gods instead of worshiping and depending on the one true God. We deny our position as dependent creatures, and we also put our dependence on people or things instead of wholly on God.

It's true, God intended us to have relationship with people, and a healthy marriage has some degree of interdependence. However, the only person who should be totally dependent on someone else to meet all his or her needs is an infant. Once an individual starts to mature, she becomes less and less dependent on one person (Mom or Dad) for her entire well-being and learns to assume some responsibility for herself. She also grows to trust that God uses a variety of people to meet some of her needs, including a spouse, but accepts that a husband will never meet all her needs or wants.

> The only person who should be totally dependent on someone else to meet all his or her needs is an infant.

Let's be honest, when we marry, many of us are not fully functioning adults (yet). When I got married at the age of twenty-three, there were many adult responsibilities I had never taken care of. I went from home to college, to graduate school, to marriage. I had never lived fully on my own. But in a healthy marriage, couples work these things out. They learn together, laugh together, grow up together, and recover from their mistakes together. They often marry someone with strengths in the very areas where they are weak and benefit from each other. But there are two types of unhealthy dependence that will cause a marriage (or any other adult relationship) to become destructive.

The first one is where *I need you to love me in order for me to be okay.* This person puts another individual in God's place as her foundational source for love and acceptance. She seeks a love object to fill her up, to complete her, to rescue her or to make her happy. She feels empty inside with no strong core of who she is. Therefore she comes to a relationship starving, looking for someone to nourish her like a baby seeks a mother or a tick seeks a dog.

Elise came to counseling, feeling suicidal after a breakup initiated by her boyfriend. She sobbed, "What did I do wrong? Why couldn't he love me?" No amount of rational talk about personality differences, his not being the right one, or God's will could soothe Elise's broken heart. His rejection of her defined her. She said, "What's wrong with me? I feel so unworthy I want to die." This kind of thinking is dangerous and destructive. Even if Elise found a man to love her, what mere mortal could fully fill her empty love tank? And when he fails (as he will), what happens to her or to him?

Watching the movie *Jerry Maguire,* women in the audience collectively swooned when Tom Cruise told Renée Zellweger, "I love you. You complete me." It's a nice line for a Hollywood movie, but don't fall for it. The truth is, if we each need someone to complete us, we won't make good marriage partners. No other human beings can complete us if we are not whole ourselves. Only God completes us.

It is quite seductive when a man whispers, "I love how you love me" or "I need you to complete me." But stop for a minute and listen to the words. The emphasis is on the word *me.* It's a selfish love because it's self-focused and toxic to the person who is being loved. It's not *I love you,* but rather *I love you loving me.* Ava was married to a man whose love started to suffocate her. She said, "I can't breathe. My husband sticks to me like a barnacle. I'm exhausted trying to meet his constant demands for reassurance, attention, and sex. There is no room in this relationship for me to be me or for him to love me. I exist to take care of him." Oswald Chambers wrote,

> If we love a human being and do not love God, we demand of
> him every perfection and every rectitude, and when we do not get
> it we become cruel and vindictive; we are demanding of a human
> being that which he or she cannot give. There is only one Being
> Who can satisfy the last aching abyss of the human heart, and
> that is the Lord Jesus Christ. Why Our Lord is apparently so
> severe regarding every human relationship is because He knows
> that every relationship not based on loyalty to Himself will end in
> disaster.[4]

A second kind of unhealthy dependency is where *I need you to need me in order for me to be okay.* The same emphasis is on the word *me* but with a slightly different bent. This kind of person often functions as a rescuer, hero, fixer, or the more capable one, when in reality, he or she is also quite needy but unaware of it. He uses people to feel better about himself. He does this by taking care of others' problems or being overly involved in people's lives, all the while staying completely blind to his own problems. This person is usually attracted to someone who is weak, vulnerable, or one who needs fixing or rescuing. The destructive thing about a fixer or rescuer is that he doesn't really want the other person to get healthy because then he or she wouldn't need him any longer. We often see this kind of dysfunctional pattern with parents who are unable to let go of their adult children, enabling them to stay weak and dependent on them because of the parent's need to be needed.

Brenda was married to a chiropractor who loved taking care of everyone, including her. He was well loved by his patients, because he took the time to listen and was readily available whenever they had a need. For Brenda, however, his hovering over her felt demeaning. He called her constantly, checking on her whereabouts and making sure she was safe. He questioned how she did things and whether or not it was the "best" way they could be done. He evaluated her diet and told her where she could make improvements to lose weight. He insisted she put socks on at the airport, because he didn't want her bare feet touching the dirty floor when they went through security.

At first she found his attention flattering, but she grew to hate it. She wanted to make her own decisions about what she ate or whether or not she wanted to put socks on during their travels, without a constant commentary about what she was doing wrong or what she could do better. Brenda often tried asserting herself, but it never ended well. Once, she told Ted that she was not going to order something on the menu just because he said it was better for her, but Ted sulked the rest of the evening, saying she didn't appreciate how much he loved her.

And, Brenda had to admit, she didn't. She felt angrier and angrier and hated being treated like a child. Sometimes she found herself acting like a compliant little girl who did whatever her daddy wanted, and then she'd switch into a rebellious teenager who talked back and wasn't going to listen at all. She loathed what was happening to herself and her marriage but didn't know how to change the unhealthy dance they both were dancing.[5] In a mature relationship, the goal is for both individuals to fully function as healthy adults. However, in a dependent relationship where one wants to fix and control someone else, attempts for independence are seen as threats to the rescuer's sense of worth and are usually squashed or undermined, creating a destructive pattern to the marriage and both individuals in the relationship.

Clinging, smothering, demanding, and controlling are the signs of unhealthy dependence in one or both partners in the marriage.

INDIFFERENCE

The opposite of love isn't hate; it is indifference. Indifference says I don't care enough about you to give you my time, my energy, or other resources to show interest, care, or love toward you.[6] Indifference says how you feel or what you want doesn't matter to me. Indifference says you are not a person to love, but an object to use. Indifference says I don't need to change anything to make our relationship better for you if it's okay for me. Indifference says that you exist for my benefit and when you don't please me or benefit me anymore, you are replaceable or disposable.[7]

One of the most horrific abuse stories in all of Scripture is one of gross marital indifference. A Levite and his concubine wife were traveling home when they stopped in the town of Gibeah for the evening. Expecting the typical Jewish hospitality, they waited in the open square of the city, hoping someone would invite them to spend the night in his or her home. As evening descended, an old man spotted the couple and graciously took them in. While the two men were enjoying getting acquainted, vile men of the city surrounded the home, beat on the door, and demanded the old man bring his guest outside so they might ravish him.

The old man pleaded, "No, my friends, don't be so vile. Since this man is my guest, don't do this disgraceful thing" (Judges 19:23). What he said next shocks us to our core. He said, "Look, here is my virgin daughter, and his concubine. I will bring them out to you now, and you can use them and do to them whatever you wish. But to this man, don't do such a disgraceful thing" (verse 24).

The men of the town refused to listen to the old man, so the Levite grabbed his concubine wife and shoved her out the door. All night long the men of the town raped her, taking turns until dawn. Broken and bleeding, she stumbled back to the doorstep where her husband slept and there she collapsed.

The Scriptures say that when her husband opened the door to leave, there lay his concubine with her hands on the threshold. He coldly said, "Get up; let's go" (verse 28). But there was no answer. He tossed her lifeless body on his donkey and took her home. Later on, he cut her up into twelve pieces and sent one piece to each of the twelve tribes of Israel, portraying himself (not his poor wife) as the victim of a horrible injustice (see Judges 19:1–30, NLT).[8]

This Levite husband chose to sacrifice his wife to ensure his own safety. When she lay broken and used up, dying on the doorstep, he showed no compassion or care for what she had just been through. He was indifferent to her torture and the pain she endured. When he saw her sprawled on the doorstep, he ordered her to get up, not realizing that she was already dead. The rape and torture by those vile men was traumatic, but I often wonder if her greater suffering was that her own husband indifferently tossed her out the door like a piece of trash, knowing full well she would be used and abused.

Marriage is the one relationship where we publicly make promises not to be indifferent. I've never attended a marriage ceremony where only one person took vows. Together and in front of God and witnesses, we promise to love, to cherish, to protect, and to honor the person we choose to marry. We may all be indifferent in minor areas at times, but when we regularly fail to keep our fundamental marital promises, the marriage is in deep trouble, and to pretend otherwise is not healthy.

Karen loved her husband and wanted things to work between them, but he had little time for her. He was busy running a business and making money, and these things took priority. When she tried to talk about her feelings, he became harsh and then refused to talk with her at all, sometimes ignoring her for months. When Karen pursued or pressured him to discuss their problems, he accused her of being controlling and manipulative. The only connection he offered her was sexual, and this left Karen feeling empty and used. Finally, for her own mental health, she decided to have a heart-to-heart talk. She hoped that once Stan saw how hurt she was, he'd begin to show some care for her. She also knew the area he'd be most receptive to improving would be their sexual relationship. Karen prayed and pondered, asking God to give her the right words to invite her husband into a different kind of relationship with her. She prepared what she wanted to say and practiced it over and over again until her tone was neither accusing nor sharp.

One evening, after wiring up all her courage, she said, "Stan, there is something I need to share with you that's really important. Do you have time tonight?"

"Okay, but I don't have all night. There's a football game starting in about fifteen minutes."

Karen took a deep breath and began. "I know you get very frustrated when I'm not responsive to your physical needs. I know you want me to be more sexual with you and enjoy our physical relationship. But the way you treat me much of the time makes me feel angry and hurt. We don't have fun together. We don't talk. I barely see you. When you're angry with me, you ignore me for long periods of time and accuse me of being things that I'm not. I just can't manufacture warm and affectionate feelings toward you when you're ready to be intimate, when there's not anything positive going on in our relationship. Wouldn't you enjoy our sexual relationship much more if you knew I wanted to be with you and that I enjoyed that part of our relationship rather than me just doing my wifely duty?"

"Of course I would," Stan said, but then briskly added, "but if wifely duty is all I can get, I'll settle for that."

Stan's indifference stung sharply, but it woke Karen up to his total lack of care for her as his wife, as a woman, and as a person. Everything in their relationship revolved around him and his needs. As long as her body was available when he wanted sex, it mattered little to him whether or not she enjoyed it or felt loved.

Being married does not give husbands the right to gratify their sexual needs apart from their commitment to the spiritual, physical, and emotional well-being of their wives. A wife is not a body to use but a person to love.

Later, Karen told me, "God used this utterly selfish response of my husband to powerfully speak into my heart—by letting me know that God desired my husband to care for me and my feelings. God never intended me to be a sexual object or to sacrifice my body to enable my husband's selfishness to continue unchallenged."

Being married does not give husbands the right to gratify their sexual needs apart from their commitment to the spiritual, physical, and emotional well-being of their wives. A wife is not a body to use but a person to love.[9]

Each one of us gets married as a sinner with baggage. If we want to have successful marriages as well as minimize lethal wounds in our closest relationships, it's important that we know what kind of baggage is in our suitcases and how much we're carrying. Each one of us is capable of any one or all these destructive attitudes and actions. But when we do them and don't see that we have—or we refuse to listen to the feedback that our respective spouses give us about how our attitudes and behaviors affect them—we are blind, and a good marriage is impossible. Bill and Pam Farrel, authors of the book *The 10 Best Decisions a Single Can Make*, describe toxic love using 1 Corinthians 13 as their guide. They wrote:

> Toxic is impatient and unkind. Toxic is always envious and jealous. Toxic boasts and is self-glorifying. Toxic is arrogant and proud, self-centered and rude. Toxic easily loses its temper and keeps track of all offenses and holds a grudge. Toxic is thrilled when people look and feel stupid. Toxic loves a mistake because she can tell everyone of the error and replay it over and over. Toxic runs to evil, never protects others, and gives up on people and life easily.[10]

Reactive abuse, controlling abuse, deceit, dependence, and indifference are not characteristics of godly love. They are destructive; and if a marriage is to be restored, they must stop.

Dear God,

Thank you for helping me see that you are for me and not against me. Thank you for giving me words to describe what's happening in my marriage and for showing me that you do not care more about marriage and men than you care about me. Help me not be afraid.

Action Step: Go back and review your test results from chapter 1. What patterns do you see most prevalent in your marriage: reactive abuse, controlling abuse, deceit, dependence, or indifference? Are there any destructive behaviors or patterns that you see yourself engaging in also?

Four

Where Is God in All of This?

Have mercy on us, LORD, have mercy,
for we have had our fill of contempt.
We have had more than our fill of the scoffing
of the proud
and the contempt of the arrogant.

—Psalm 123:3–4, NLT

Recently, I received an e-mail from a woman in a destructive marriage. Jamie wrote,

Leslie, I don't know what's happening to me. Every day I thank
God that he's kept me sane in this web of chaos, anger, and deceit,
but I'm starting to lose it. I'm having heart palpitations, I feel sick
to my stomach, I can't think straight, and I'm scared, angry, and
hurt all the time.

Despite my husband's lack of any type of remorse, I stand
on the truth of God's Word and take my marital vows seriously!
I don't want a divorce…BUT how much can one person take?
I feel like I am going CRAZY! The more Christian wisdom I
seek, the more confused I become.

I don't want to manipulate God's Word for my benefit or to

relieve myself from this pain or journey. But surely God does not require that we live in this type of hell simply to remain faithful to our marriage vows, does he? Am I forever damned to this marriage?

I have sought much Christian guidance and, sad to say, it has been horribly ineffective and more damaging, which leads me back to the place I started. I don't want to break the vow I made to God in this marriage, and yet I am trapped in a marriage that I am trying to survive while dying more every day. What is the answer?

Surely I am more to God than just a sacrificial lamb! I am very ashamed that this is my life and more deeply ashamed that I find myself in this predicament. I am not looking for an easy way out.... I want out through the way of the truth (whatever that looks like). But the darkness has become so dense I cannot find the light!

This woman's words echo the desperate cry of many Christian wives who feel trapped, hopeless, and helpless. They've prayed, they've pleaded, they've nagged, they've raged, they've repented, they've read Christian books, they've fasted, and they've gotten biblical counsel. They've done all they know to do—and more—to make their marriages better, but nothing changes. It is indeed a treacherous path to walk through, especially if we cannot find the light. As a lighthouse is to a lost sailor in a stormy sea, God and his Word provide that light for us to look at so that we can see clearly what's happening, who we are, what to do, and how to respond. The psalmist says, "For with you is the fountain of life; in your light we see light" (Psalm 36:9, NIV).

Perhaps you've been hurt by poor counsel, or misunderstood and maligned by church leaders for the stand you've taken. Maybe you think that God is more interested in preserving your marriage than the well-being of you and your children, but that is not true. God values marriage, but he's also concerned for your safety and sanity in the midst of a destructive and/or dangerous marriage. The psalmist cried in the midst of being oppressed, "Guide my steps by your word, so I will not be overcome by evil" (Psalm 119:133, NLT).

It's easy for people to take a sentence from the Bible like "I hate divorce" (Malachi 2:16, NLT) and make a definitive statement about what to do in every circumstance. But I think it's wiser and more biblical to look at the whole picture of who God is and how he feels about situations like you are in.

As we seek God's help right now, it's very important to be anchored to some crucial truths from Scripture. It's easy for people to take a sentence from the Bible like "I hate divorce" (Malachi 2:16, NLT) and make a definitive statement about what to do in every circumstance. But I think it's wiser and more biblical to look at the whole picture of who God is and how he feels about situations like you are in. He also has things to say to you in the midst of your suffering to give you help and hope. To navigate through this darkness, it is important you know that God is not only for marriage, but he is for people, and for women. He is for you and loves you with an everlasting love. He does not ask you to be the sacrificial lamb; he already provided one. Jesus. Let him show you the way to walk through this darkness.

God Knows How You Feel

It's hard for some people to imagine that the God of the universe, the God who is all knowing and all powerful, has emotions and feels sad, hurt, and rejected—but he does. When we look at the Old Testament story, we see a God who created human beings in his likeness, including having emotions. He created Adam and Eve and blessed them with everything they needed or wanted. He gave them a beautiful environment to live in, a companion to enjoy life with, and a purpose to take care of his creation. Yet Adam's and Eve's hearts weren't completely content. The serpent zeroed in on what he thought would lure them into his trap. Satan tempted Eve to want something more than God had already provided. Instead of being satisfied with their status as creatures, Satan tempted them with the opportunity to be godlike, in knowing good from evil. First Eve, then Adam, fell for the lie that God must have cheated them from something more when he instructed them not to eat from the Tree of the Knowledge of Good and Evil. Once they ate, however, they realized that they'd been duped. They didn't get more; they now had less. Instead of freedom and intimacy, they now felt shame and guilt—emotions they had never experienced before. Instead of feeling safe and secure with each other and with God, they now felt afraid. Instead of turning to God, they now ran and hid.

God loved Adam and Eve and felt hurt and disappointed when they chose to believe the serpent, and not trust him. That was the start of God's heartbreak over the human race. People's sin and corruption only grew worse. By Genesis chapter 6, it says, "The LORD saw that the wickedness of man was great in the earth, and that every intention of the thoughts of his heart was only evil continually. And the LORD regretted that he had made man on the earth, and it *grieved* him to his heart" (verses 5–6). Similarly, God sees that you are grieved to the heart with the state of your marriage, your husband's choices, and that you are perhaps even sorry that you ever married him in the first place. Don't feel afraid of being honest with God about how you feel. He understands that kind of pain and anguish.

Once again in the Old Testament, God reached out for a relationship with a group of individuals to be his own special people. Through Abraham's seed, God invited the Jews into an exclusive covenant relationship with him, much like a marriage.[1] There were promises made to love, to be faithful, and to be exclusive, just like in marriage. God wanted them to enjoy his love and love him in return (see Deuteronomy 6:5). He promised his faithfulness and required they be faithful in return (see Deuteronomy 4:23–24). But once again God's heart got broken. Israel didn't choose to love God first or the most. She ran after other lovers and repeatedly broke her promises to God. She was rebellious, ungrateful, self-absorbed, and forgot him. Israel became indifferent to the promises she had made to God and their covenant relationship. She took God for granted and used him to help her when she was in trouble, but didn't honor, love, or respect him. Does that sound like your marriage? God knows how you feel.

Throughout much of the Old Testament, we see God pleading for Israel to return to him, to repent, to wake up and change her ways. And yet, time and time again the Scriptures tell us that she refused to listen. She refused to love him or honor him as God in her life, and God's heart was broken. Much of the book of Jeremiah is God lamenting over Israel's rejection and his broken heart (see Jeremiah 1–6 for a potent description of this).

Jesus, too, understands how you feel. He was physically abused, disrespected, humiliated, beaten, lied about, accused, mocked, reviled, spit upon, and unjustly treated by religious and political leaders who misused their power and authority. Throughout Christ's time on earth, his goal was for people to see God's heart. He wanted to show them what God was truly like (see John 1:18; Colossians 1:15; Hebrews 1:3). Time after time, Jesus pleaded with people to repent and return to God as their first love. Most of them refused. In a moment of heartbreak, Jesus cried,

"O Jerusalem, Jerusalem, the city that kills the prophets and stones those who are sent to it! How often would I have gathered your children together as a hen gathers her brood under her wings, and *you were not willing*!" (Luke 13:34).

Jesus's cry underscores the important element of choice in all relationships, even our relationship with God. Although God and Jesus want a close, loving relationship with people, it doesn't happen if we are unwilling to repent and return to him. There isn't anyone who could be more appealing, loving, desirable, and worthy of love than Jesus; yet as we see in the passage above, there were many who chose not to love or follow him.

When you are rejected or unloved, disrespected or abused, it is awful and hurts you deeply, but it is not a statement about who you are. It doesn't mean you are unworthy of love or care any more than the rejection of Jesus meant he was unworthy of love and respect.

God knows how you feel, but please understand that when you are rejected or unloved, disrespected or abused, it is awful and hurts you deeply, but it is not a statement about who you are. It doesn't mean you are unworthy of love or care any more than the rejection of Jesus meant he was unworthy of love and respect. In this time of pain, run to God because he knows exactly how you feel.

GOD HATES WHAT'S HAPPENING IN DESTRUCTIVE MARRIAGES

Let's go back to Jamie's situation. Jamie has gone to her pastors for advice, and now she's getting more and more confused. Her husband has not technically committed adultery, so her pastor tells her that she has no biblical grounds for divorce. Yet Jamie knows her husband masturbates to porn movies on their marital bed. He has not left the home, but he will not work regularly to provide an income that will support them. When Jamie confronts him, he gets defensive and lies. When she challenges him, she gets ignored for long periods of time. She desperately desires to honor her marriage vows, but she can only do her part. Marriage is a relationship where two people make promises and commitments. When one breaks his or her promises or is faithless, the relationship fractures. The good news is that the fracture can be healed through confession, personal repentance, and forgiveness. The bad news is that without those things, the marriage can never be what God intends, and God doesn't ask you to pretend otherwise.

Sin damages relationships. You only have to start reading in Genesis to see the truth of this. Cain killed Abel. Joseph's brothers sold Joseph into slavery. Rebekah manipulated Isaac and Jacob into stealing Esau's birthright, and Esau held a grudge against Jacob for years. Laban lied to Jacob and treated his daughters as if they were objects. As a result, Leah lived in a loveless marriage, hoping that children would make her husband love her. We could go on and on, but I think it's clear. God allowed the unvarnished stories of flawed and broken people in the Scriptures for us to realize how damaging sin is. As we've already seen, God made a sacred covenant with the Jewish people, but when Israel and Judah left God to worship idols, their relationship with God broke. After much anguish and pleading and waiting, God gave them a certificate of divorce, while still longing and hoping for their heartfelt repentance. He did not want their lip service or a going-through-the-motions kind of relationship; he wanted genuine love and repentance (see Jeremiah 3:6–14).

God wants that for people, too, when they have been sinned against. Throughout Scripture he tells us how to make amends, make restitution, and reconcile broken relationships. But it doesn't happen without humility, confession, and change. People who have been deeply sinned against or betrayed don't want mere lip service or someone superficially going through the motions of change any more than God does; they want to see real effort and genuine change.

Let's look at the greater context of what God is saying in the oft-quoted passage in Malachi about divorce. Throughout the entire Old Testament, God uses marriage as a word picture to describe his covenantal relationship with the Jews. In Malachi, the larger story was God's rebuke of Judah's unfaithfulness and his call for her full repentance. Malachi said,

> Here is another thing you do. You cover the LORD's altar with tears, weeping and groaning because he pays no attention to your offerings and doesn't accept them with pleasure. You cry out, "Why doesn't the LORD accept my worship?" I'll tell you why! Because the LORD witnessed the vows you and your wife made when you were young. But you have been unfaithful to her, though she remained your faithful partner, the wife of your marriage vows.
>
> Didn't the LORD make you one with your wife? In body and spirit you are his. And what does he want? Godly children from your union. So guard your heart; remain loyal to the wife of your youth. "For I hate divorce!" says the LORD, the God of Israel. "To divorce your wife is to overwhelm her with cruelty," says the LORD of Heaven's Armies. "So guard your heart; do not be unfaithful to your wife." (2:13–16, NLT)

In this passage, what God hates is when a husband has been treacherous and unfaithful to his wife. God hates when her husband overwhelms her with cruelty because of the hardness of his heart. God hates when her husband treats her disdainfully by throwing her away like a piece of trash when he tires of her.

When a couple enters into the covenant of marriage, they each make promises to be sexually exclusive as well as to faithfully provide, protect, and care for each other. Unfaithfulness in marriage doesn't only occur in the sexual realm. It happens when there is a regular pattern of not caring, not providing, not protecting, and not honoring. Unfaithfulness is leaving the marriage relationship even when you haven't physically left the home or even the marital bed.

Unfaithfulness in marriage doesn't only occur in the sexual realm. It happens when there is a regular pattern of not caring, not providing, not protecting, and not honoring. Unfaithfulness is leaving the marriage relationship even when you haven't physically left the home or even the marital bed.

Unfaithfulness is a term God used throughout the Old Testament to describe Israel's and Judah's abandonment of their relationship with God. *Idolatry* and *adultery* are other words he used. *Hardness of heart* is the phrase both Moses and Jesus used to describe why marriages often end. This was not God's plan for his relationship with the Jews, or for marriage, but because of sin and hardness of heart, it is a sad reality.

God Values Your Safety and Sanity

It may surprise you, but God values your safety as much if not more than you do. For example, in spite of God's general instructions to submit to the laws of the land and to higher authorities, when David feared for his life because of King Saul's jealous rages, God didn't instruct David to submit to the king and trust God to take care of him. Instead, David fled, always respecting the position of King Saul, but not allowing himself to be abused by him. (Read 1 Samuel 18–31 for the story.)

In another example, when Jesus was born and King Herod sought to exterminate all the Jewish babies two years and younger, God told Joseph in a dream to flee to Egypt until it was safe to return (see Matthew 2:13–15). When Rahab hid the Jewish spies, she lied to the soldiers in order to keep them safe, but God commended her (see Hebrews 11:31). I suspect those who lied to keep Jews safe from the Nazi army were equally commended by God when they got to heaven.

Jesus himself valued safety. He stayed away from certain places and people because he knew they meant to harm him (see John 7:1).[2] Jesus also challenged the Pharisees' legalistic application of Sabbath rules by asking them who wouldn't break the rules of the Sabbath to rescue a child or an ox that had fallen into a well (see Luke 14:5).[3] Safety is an important component of trust, especially in marriage. One of the blessings of a virtuous spouse is that you trust that he or she will do you good, not harm, all the days of your life (see Proverbs 31:12). There can be no freedom or honest communication when we feel afraid or have been threatened—physically, emotionally, or both—or if we have a price to pay whenever we honestly share our thoughts and feelings.

Women feel guilty taking measures to protect themselves, because they've been taught it's unbiblical or ungodly. Perhaps their Christian friends or church leaders have told them they have no biblical right to safety and they must stay in the marital homes, no matter what. They suffer endlessly with verbal battering and even physical abuse, believing that by doing so, they're being godly martyrs or fulfilling a call to be the sacrificial lamb. Keeping the family together at all costs is seen as God's highest value. But there are times when keeping the family together has an extremely high price for a woman and her children, and it may actually cost them their lives. In addition, staying together regardless of the costs continues to enable the husband to grossly sin against them with no consequences, which is not biblical. Proverbs 27:12 teaches us, "The prudent see danger and take refuge" (NIV). If you don't feel safe in your marriage, there is no possibility of having the kind of marriage that God intended until that issue is addressed and changed.

Sanity is also an important value to God. By sanity I don't just mean good mental health from a secular point of view, but good mental health from God's point of view. The writer of Proverbs warns us of the consequences of living with a contentious and argumentative person (see Proverbs 15:4; 17:1; 25:24; 26:28). The Scriptures are clear. People influence and affect us in both good and bad ways. When someone lives with an abusive, destructive, manipulative, and/or deceitful person, it definitely takes its toll on his or her mental, emotional, physical, and spiritual health.[4]

Being sane from God's perspective involves knowing, believing, and walking in the truth. Jesus said, "Walk while you have the light, lest darkness overtake you. The one who walks in the darkness does not know where he is going" (John 12:35). The apostle Paul says by nature we exchange the truth of God for a lie and in so doing, our minds become desecrated (see Romans 1:25–28).

Walking in light and truth are important values of God. When you live with someone who prefers deceit and darkness and who twists and manipulates the truth, it can be very stressful, confusing, crazy, and damaging to you and your children's emotions, cognitions, and physical health.

No one lives in your house with your spouse but you and your children. Therefore no one can fully see what you see or experience what you experience. No one knows how bad it hurts except you. People can tell you what they think you should do, but if you feel unsafe, please take measures to get safe.[5] If you feel like you are at the end of your rope or your ability to cope, ask for help. Even if everyone else thinks you are overreacting or stepping out of God's best, listen to your heart and gut and the Holy Spirit, and do what you need to do.

I remember when I was pregnant with our first child, all my friends told me natural childbirth was the way to go. After several of my girlfriends succeeded at drug-free births, my goal was to deliver our child without the help of any medication. "No drugs for my baby," I proudly announced to my friends and family. I knew this was obviously God's best. Yet toward the end of a very hard labor, my body was exhausted and I felt like I was at the end of my rope. I prayed, and then I screamed at the doctor, "I need drugs, *now!*" After Ryan was born, I struggled with guilt and shame. I told myself I should have tried harder to stick it out, I should have been stronger, I should have been able to do what all my friends did. Yet upon reflection I realized that my birth experience was mine. My body had a different pain threshold than my friends, and when I reached my limit, I just couldn't go on. I needed help, and God provided the doctor to help me get through that experience. If you are at your limit, reach out for help. You don't have to do this all alone.

Dear God,

It's surprising for me to see how much you care about what's happening to me and my marriage. It's comforting to me to know that you care about my safety and my sanity. But I don't know how much more I can take. Sometimes it feels like I'm at the end of my limit, but I don't know what else to do. I don't want to take drugs or have to stay on antidepressants the rest of my life just to stay married. Show me the way to get through this. Lead me to the right people who will help me.

Action Step: Make a commitment to yourself that you are going to get sane and safe and that you are not going to let this destructive marriage push you into unhealthy and sinful behaviors of your own. Pick one specific thing you could start today. For example: Start exercising. Drink more water. Eat less sugar. Join a Bible study. Develop a safety plan.

PART 2

Change Begins with You

But let us who live in the light
be clearheaded, protected by
the armor of faith and love,
and wearing as our helmet the
confidence of our salvation.

1 Thessalonians 5:8, NLT

Five

What's Wrong with Me?

My soul has dwelt too long
With one who hates peace.
I am for peace;
But when I speak, they are for war.

—Psalm 120:6–7, NKJV

Joanne called and asked, "How soon can I get in to see you?" I could hear the desperation in her voice. Several years prior I had spoken with her around some hurtful incidents in her marriage, but she wasn't quite ready to hear what I had to say to her. Most of what I remembered was Joanne making excuses for her husband's behavior.

When she previously told me Darryl had smashed all her favorite knickknacks and thrown them in the trash, she minimized his actions and said, "He's just tired of my clutter." When he threw his uneaten dinner in the sink because he said it tasted like garbage, Joanne told me, "He's under a lot of stress at work." Joanne tried to put a positive spin on her husband's actions. She loved Darryl and told herself that love always believes the best about someone. After another one of Darryl's verbal battering episodes, Joanne said, "He doesn't mean to be cruel; he's just oblivious to other people's feelings."

When I saw Joanne this time, she looked haggard and worn out. Her eyes had lost their sparkle. "I really need help right now," she whispered. "I don't want to do the wrong thing, but I know I have to do something different."

"Tell me what's brought you to this place," I said, anxious to hear what had changed Joanne's perspective.

She said, "Last week Darryl and I went for a walk, like we often do in the evenings after supper. I really didn't want to go and was anxious to get home. I had a lot of paperwork to finish before bed. I was walking slightly faster than he was. I knew he didn't like it, but when he grabbed the back of my shirt collar and yanked me to his side like a dog on a leash, something inside of me snapped. I knew that I had to start standing up for myself. Not only because he treated me as if I had no dignity or value, but in that moment I realized that it was true—I don't. I've allowed him to disrespect and degrade me all these years without protest or consequence. What's wrong with me?"

Joanne's question is an excellent place to start if we want to get healthier. Instead of focusing on what's wrong with our husbands or what he needs to change right now (which we have almost zero control over), it's important for us to take time to figure out a little more about what's going on in our own minds and hearts and what we truly want. Perhaps you haven't been passive and fearful of rocking the boat like Joanne was. You have tried to speak up about how you've been mistreated or about what's happening in your marriage. Yet nothing has changed with your husband or your marriage. But you do notice you're changing. Joanne confessed to me that although she never directly challenged Darryl's behavior, she was becoming more and more resentful and saw herself lashing out toward her children. Maybe that's your story too. Or perhaps you're getting more and more anxious and depressed, shut down, and burned out. Even *you* don't like who you are anymore.

The Bible is very clear that people who are closest to us have a strong influence on our attitudes and actions. For example, we're told not to associate with angry people because they will rub off on us and we'll become angrier too (see Proverbs 22:24–25). When we keep company with those prone to violence, we will also be more prone to those paths (see Proverbs 1:10–15; 16:29). The apostle Paul tells us that when we hang around people with low morals, they will drag us down to their level (see 1 Corinthians 15:33). When we're married to a destructive person, we, too, may become destructive toward ourselves and others. Changing these patterns can start with you, even if you are not ready to have a conversation with your husband yet. I want to give you some ways to look within and see yourself clearer. Taking the time to do these exercises will empower you to get stronger and saner. It is only then you will have the wisdom and courage to know what the next steps are to take in your marriage.

CHANGE REQUIRES SELF-AWARENESS

After Adam and Eve ate the forbidden fruit in the Garden of Eden, God asked them a question, "Where are you?" (Genesis 3:9). God did not ask them this question because he didn't know where they were. He knew exactly where they were, hiding out in the bushes, naked, ashamed, and afraid. He asked them the question so that *they* would know where they were. Adam and Eve weren't only hiding from God; they were hiding from themselves.

Self-awareness is an essential skill we must learn if we want to grow, change, and have a good relationship with God and others. The folly of fools is deceit—including the deceit of one's own self. However, we do not become aware of ourselves all by ourselves. That's impossible. As we've already learned, our natural tendency is to have blind spots about ourselves and to believe lies over truth. We (and our spouses) need the help of God's Word and the feedback from wise people to help us see and think clearly about who we are, what our strengths and weaknesses are, how we impact others, and what areas of our lives need improvement or change if we want loving connection with others.

Remember, in chapter 3 I talked about the strategy of isolation in controlling abuse. When one person seeks to be the sole source of feedback on the value, worth, strengths, weaknesses, personhood, and identity of the other, it can become quite destructive to that individual. Little by little the person you were has been chipped away, and the person that's left is not someone you like very much, but you are now too weak and worn out to resist. As a result you are fragile and easily manipulated and controlled like Joanne.

> Little by little the person you were has been chipped away, and the person that's left is not someone you like very much, but you are now too weak and worn out to resist.

Thankfully Joanne had a small but godly group of women friends who recognized what was happening and tried to speak into her life. For a long time she resisted what they said because if she believed them, she would be forced to face some ugly truths about her marriage and why she allowed herself to be abused. But one day after Bible study, she overheard one of her friends say to the other, "I'm worried about her. She's not herself anymore. She's disappeared in her marriage." Joanne felt hurt, but she knew her friend spoke the truth. She realized that to love her husband the way he wanted her to love him required that she silently lose herself. She admitted that she had allowed her identity and value to rest on what Darryl thought and said of her. She was his sexual partner, his maid, his walking companion, and his encourager, but he didn't invite her to be his partner or biblical helpmate. When she failed in her assigned role, her value diminished in Darryl's eyes and also in her own. This wake-up call of self-awareness came as a result of her overhearing her friend's words coupled with the experience of disrespect on the walk with her husband. She realized that she gave Darryl way too much power to determine her value and her worth.

When you give someone the power to define you, as Joanne did, you also give them the power to destroy you. Even if your husband devalues you, you must not devalue yourself. Why not? Because your husband is not the final word on your personhood and worth. God is.

CHANGE HAPPENS WHEN WE BELIEVE GOD'S WORDS ABOVE ALL ELSE

One of my favorite Bible stories I share with women who are ruled by what other people think of them is found in the gospel of Mark. Jesus had already chosen the twelve disciples, and the crowds were fast following him because word spread that he healed people. Yet there wasn't total agreement as to who Jesus was. The text says, "When his family heard what was happening, they tried to take him away. 'He's out of his mind,' they said. But the teachers of religious law who had arrived from Jerusalem said, 'He's possessed by Satan, the prince of demons'" (Mark 3:21–22, NLT). And yet others were amazed and said over and over again, "Everything he does is wonderful. He even makes the deaf to hear and gives speech to those who cannot speak" (Mark 7:37, NLT). Whose interpretation is right? Is Jesus crazy as his family said? demon possessed as the religious leaders said? Or is he as wonderful as the ones who were healed said? Jesus was not controlled by his approval ratings nor was his identity defined by what people said about him. He knew who he was because he believed what God said.

Your core value does not rest on the words of your husband or your mother or your father or your children or even your best friend. It rests on

God's words because he's the only one who will always tell you the truth all the time. People change. They fail. They lie. Their knowledge is limited, their thinking distorted, and their hearts are not always pure or good. Therefore it's dangerous to allow them to determine your worth. Yes, it feels great when people love us and think we're wonderful, but it is also devastating when they don't. When you depend on human beings to define your identity or determine your worth, you're in for a rocky ride and you will never be stable or healthy.

Please believe the truth: God loves you. He loves you whether or not you believe him, but you will feel much differently inside when you do believe him. Thirty years ago, we adopted a baby girl from Korea. We named her Amanda Lin and loved her as much as we loved our biological son, Ryan. We immediately changed our will to ensure her safety and security as our daughter if something were to happen to us. Growing up, she had the same blessings and privileges of being our daughter and living in our home as our biological son did. Yet as Amanda got older, her emotional security and internal well-being depended on whether she believed that was true and trusted us. If she refused to believe or wavered in her trust, our love for her would stay the same, but her sense of security and stability would vanish. She'd know we loved her in her head, but not with her heart.

Many Christians know God's love intellectually, but not experientially. When that happens, the result is insecurity and instability in our relationship with God. The disciple John knew how important it was for us to believe that God loves us. He wrote, "So we have come to know and to *believe* the love that God has for us. God is love, and whoever abides in love abides in God, and God abides in him" (1 John 4:16). Believing is a lifelong process and sometimes hard work, yet it's so worth the struggle because once you can believe God's words over the noise of everyone else's words, healing comes quickly (see Psalm 107:20).

It's important for you to know that God designed you from scratch and knows who he made you to become (see Psalm 139). He values you so much that he came to earth as a human being to rescue you from darkness and bring light and life to your soul (see Colossians 1:13–20). He is for you not against you (see Romans 8:31). When you receive his forgiveness, he adopts you as his very own daughter and now sees you as holy, blameless, and without fault (see Colossians 1:21–22). Even when you're still all messed up inside, he sees the good he put inside of you as well as all your gifts and abilities (even if you can't see them yet). He has a plan for your life, and he wants to bring wholeness and healing to your mind and your heart. He has not only forgiven you from the penalty of sin, but rescued you from the power of sin. You are now free to say yes to God and no to sin. He promises to give you wisdom whenever you ask for it (see James 1:5). He will help you live your life to please him and fulfill your purpose, but understand that in doing so you will not always make everyone around you happy. But you will be in good company. Jesus couldn't make everyone happy. He didn't even try.

CHANGE HAPPENS WHEN WE SEEK AND RECEIVE FEEDBACK FROM WISE AND GODLY PEOPLE

In addition to God and the Bible, we need reflection from others to help us become more aware and to see ourselves more clearly. I remember speaking at a large event several years ago. Exiting the bathroom, just before I took the stage, a woman grabbed me from behind. She discreetly informed me that the back corner of my skirt was tucked into my stockings. Not a pretty scene and one that would have embarrassed me greatly if I had gotten to the stage in that condition. I was thankful she took the time to approach a total stranger and make me aware of what I could not see myself.

Other women have blessed me when they've shared the good things they've seen in me or reminded me of my gifts and strengths. Virelle encouraged me as a young writer to pursue my passion. She told me God had indeed gifted me when I was questioning that calling. On the other hand, there are times it's important that we are open to negative feedback as well. Carla told me that I intimidated people, which completely floored me and wounded my ego. I had no idea she saw me as intimidating. Yet her comment helped me. It made me more aware that my quiet and reserved personality may be seen by others as arrogance and may seem intimidating.

Please be careful whose feedback you invite and take to heart. As we've already seen, there are people who will either tell us what we want to hear or try to hurt us with lies. I'd encourage you to ask a few people to be honest with you. People who will let you know when their experience of you is different than you think it is. Having trusted truth tellers in our lives is one way we can keep from being unaware or self-deceived.

Change Happens When We Take Responsibility for Our Part of the Marital Dysfunction

It's tempting to feel like a victim and to blame your spouse for everything that's wrong in your marriage. But if you want to change things and get healthy, you must take time to look at yourself first. Have you been too passive? Perhaps you've overfunctioned and allowed your husband to underfunction and now you're not happy with that arrangement, but instead of having a mature discussion, you've begun criticizing and belittling him. Has your heart grown resentful and bitter and in anger you've lashed out, but then gone back to the same patterns because you've felt guilty for the way you handled things?

He may be 100 percent responsible for his tongue or temper, but if your marriage has been rocky and unhappy, you have a part to play in that as well. Look over the history of your relationship from the first time you met until the present. Was it always destructive? If not, when did it start to change? Was it after children? Have there been some exceptional stressors in your relationship such as posttraumatic stress from serving in the armed forces, job layoffs, financial crisis, mental health issues, extended-family interference? Women who feel disappointed in their marriages often realize that in their sadness and hurt, they've become critical and contemptuous toward their husbands, often belittling their weaknesses and disrespecting them in front of the children. What once were C-minus marriages have grown into D-minus marriages, or worse, partly because of their own sinful response to marital disappointment and suffering.

CHANGE REQUIRES SELF-REFLECTION

The Bible encourages us to "give careful thought to your ways" (Haggai 1:7, NIV). There are many individuals who come up blank when asked the questions, "What are you feeling?" "What do you think about that?" "What do you really want in life?" "What are your core values?" Questions about feelings, thoughts, and values can cause some people to feel anxious because they really don't know themselves very well.

The writer of Proverbs tells us that "the wisdom of the prudent is to understand his [or her] way" (Proverbs 14:8, NKJV). It takes time and energy to be quiet and reflect about who you are, what you think, how you feel, what's important to you, and what you want (or don't want). Some people think those kinds of questions are self-indulgent and self-centered. However, it's important we understand that we can't let anyone else know who we are or where we are unless we ourselves know. Selfishness isn't characterized by knowing how you feel or what you want; selfishness is when you demand that other people always cater to your feelings, your wants, and your needs.

> Selfishness isn't characterized by knowing how you feel or what you want; selfishness is when you demand that other people always cater to your feelings, your wants, and your needs.

To grow in self-reflection, ask yourself "what" questions. Don't just swallow what everyone tells you, but ask yourself what you think about a certain topic or current event. When something painful happens, ask yourself what feelings are coming up inside. Are you scared? sad? angry? shamed? Do you know how to tell the difference? Sometimes we have a difficult time identifying our feelings or even admitting to having them, but it's a crucial skill if we are going to have intimate relationships and good emotional and spiritual health.

Journaling can be an excellent way to reflect upon your day's experiences. Don't just write about what happened; write about how you thought about what happened and what you felt and even what you wanted. Then read it back and ask yourself if there is anything more inside you that you need to know. Then write what comes out. That will give you good practice in getting to know yourself and reflecting on what comes to the surface.

Change Requires Self-Examination

The word *examine* means to study or scrutinize something more closely. Plato said, "The unexamined life is not worth living." The apostle Paul tells us to examine ourselves before partaking in communion, so that we will not be careless or reckless with this sacred sacrament (see 1 Corinthians 11:28). Most self-examination questions begin with "Why?" For example, the psalmist asked himself, "Why are you cast down, O my soul, and why are you in turmoil within me?" (Psalm 42:5).

Once you become aware that you have a certain feeling, ask yourself, "Why is it here? What purpose does it serve?" Our emotions are meant to inform us, not rule us. Our emotions always serve a purpose, like the warning lights on a car dashboard. Ignoring them doesn't make them go away, and often ignoring our feelings only makes the problem worse. For example, when we refuse to admit to ourselves that we're angry or depressed, jealous or sad, shamed or afraid, we can't take the next step of deciding what (if anything) we want to do about those emotions. And if we don't decide what to do with our emotions, our emotions will rule us, sometimes in the most hurtful and inappropriate ways. When you live with a toxic person, it's easy to become full of negative, toxic emotions of your own. If we don't pay attention and see what's happening to our own spirits and behavior, we will only make things worse in our marriages and begin our own downward spirals of resentment, bitterness, and even depression and self-hatred.

As Joanne did the work of becoming more aware, she faced some painful truths about herself and her marriage. She realized that her husband wasn't the only one who needed to change. She saw that she lived as a people pleaser and had a difficult time tolerating people's disappointment in her. She often said yes, when she knew in her heart she should say no. Once she examined herself, she realized that her love for Darryl wasn't biblical love but rather an unhealthy dependency coupled with fear. Over the years she anxiously placated him and made excuses for his behaviors because she was afraid of conflict and of being unloved and alone. But her choices cost her and her family. She sacrificed her personhood, her dignity, her and her children's safety, and her husband's growth.

You might be a little apprehensive to see in yourself what you've ignored for so long. It's like stepping on the scale after avoiding it for the last six months (or six years), knowing the news is not good but afraid of just how bad it will be. But if you want things to be different, you must look, because awareness is the precursor to action. We can't change what we won't see or admit. If awareness doesn't lead to action, then it brings despair rather than hope.

If you want to have a meaningful life or work toward reversing a destructive marriage, ask yourself what changes need to be made, starting with you. A great place to start your change process is by putting your marriage in its proper place.

Change Requires Putting Your Marriage in Its Proper Place

You might be thinking that if you want your marriage to get better, you'll have to put your husband first and make your marriage your number one priority. But that's not what I'm going to tell you. In fact, one of the reasons your marriage has gotten this bad is that, like Joanne, your marriage has been too important to you. You've already read stories of women who have sacrificed their safety, their sanity, their personhood, and their children's well-being in order to keep their marriages together at all costs, at any price.

Joanne realized that her marriage, although important to her, had become idolatrous. Keeping it together was what controlled her, not the love of Christ. Joanne confessed, "I now see that I was so absorbed in preserving my marriage that I've lived by fear and not by faith. I was so caught up in making sure I was making Darryl happy and keeping the peace, I've not loved him well at all. I allowed his behavior to go unchallenged. He's not only hurt me and the children; he's hurt himself. He's not anything like the man God wants him to be."

Recognizing Marriage as an Idol

How can you tell whether or not your marriage has become an idol (too important)? The biggest red flag is when you fall into deep despair or panic when your husband fails to love you well. For example, what happens to you and in you when your husband disappoints you over and over again? when he doesn't treat you like you want him to? when he won't stay present and work things out during a conflict? when he lies or cheats on you or mistreats you? Any wife would feel disappointed, hurt, and angry. But if you find yourself becoming increasingly despairing, fearful, controlling, or resentful, it's time to pay attention. Those negative emotions are a good indicator that your desire for a good marriage has become too important. It's become an idol. As we learned in chapter 3, whenever we are dependent on something or someone other than God, it will always hurt us.

> One of the reasons your marriage has gotten this bad
> is that your marriage has been too important to you.

Center Yourself in God, Not in Your Spouse

Women have been groomed to put marriage first, as their highest purpose and deepest desire. But that's not biblical. God wants to be our first love, and he wants our primary purpose to be to know and glorify him. Jesus commands us to love God first, with everything we have, not only because God deserves our love and is worthy of it, but because he knows how crucial it is to our long-term well-being. God knows that whatever we love the most will rule our lives. That's why the Bible counsels us to let the love of Christ control us (see 2 Corinthians 5:14), not the love of lesser things. Desiring a good marriage is not wrong. The problem comes when we place marriage above all else, including God. The human heart craves more than human solutions, human love, or even biblical principles. It needs to fall more deeply in love with God.

As you learn to center yourself in God's love and not your husband, you are no longer debilitated when your spouse fails you or disappoints you. Yes, you hurt, but you are centered and controlled by something other than your marriage or your man. You have received from God the strength and courage to both forgive your spouse for his sinful failings as well as set appropriate boundaries and consequences when he continues to be unrepentant and destructive to the marriage and to you. With God as your first love, you can love and be compassionate without being foolish and enabling because God shows you how to love in a way that is in the best interest of your husband. In loving your husband well, you trust God with the outcome of your marriage.

Let me ask you a question. If you do your part and your marriage doesn't make it, can you trust God to be enough for you? You must settle this question deep in your heart because until you do, you will be too afraid to make the changes you need to make. As you start to do things differently, the destructive marital boat you're on will start to rock and there are no guarantees that it will right itself. But I do know one thing for sure. When your marriage has been in a downward spiral of dangerous sin and destruction, and everything you've tried up to now has not resulted in any lasting positive change, it's time to change your strategy.

There are times you must risk unraveling the life you have in order to create the life God wants for you.

Dear God,

I see myself in Joanne's story. I never realized my part in this destructive marriage, and I want to change. I don't want to let it destroy me or my family, but I don't know how to change and I still feel afraid to see, to change, to do something different. Lord, give me the wisdom I need to become more aware of my own part before I even think about talking to my husband about his part.

Action Step: What are some of your internal fears and lies that you must now become more aware of? These lies and fears have kept you stuck in your own unhealthy patterns and silent in your marriage. They have kept you from speaking up or making a change. For example, a fear might be, *I'm afraid of being alone.* A lie might be, *No one would ever believe me if I revealed what's happening at home.*

Fears	Lies
_____	_____
_____	_____
_____	_____

What is something you could do that would help you face one of your fears and challenge one specific lie this week?

Six

When Trying Harder Becomes Destructive

If I am no good to him, if I am merely a doll, a *wife*, and not a *human being*—then it is all useless and I don't want to carry on this existence.

—Sophie Tolstoy, wife of Leo Tolstoy

A my leaned forward, her lips slowly parting to say something. She stopped herself and fell back in her chair, confusion written all over her face. Finally she said, "I can hardly believe what I'm now seeing. All these years I've tried so hard to be everything I thought Charlie wanted me to be. Everything I thought God wanted me to be. I desperately tried to be a good wife, to get it right. And now I see that I only enabled his selfishness to grow into a monster."

I nodded, watching Amy absorb what she said.

"I made our marriage worse by never speaking up, by being too nice, by not expressing my needs, and by accommodating Charlie even at my own expense. I went along thinking that this was my role as a godly woman, a submissive wife, a biblical helpmate. I'm so angry. How could I have been so wrong?"

For a long time Christian wives have been counseled to do exactly what Amy (and Joanne from chapter 5) tried in order to fix their marriages or make them better. They've been told to try harder to be more submissive, more caring, more respectful, more attentive to their husbands' needs, more positive and encouraging, and less demanding. In many marriages, this might be good counsel. When you begin to sincerely try harder to meet someone's needs, be more respectful, or humbly apologize, it usually begets a reciprocal response in the other person. He begins to try harder too, and he is also sorry. Amends are made and the relationship is repaired. This is a good start, and someone needs to get the ball rolling. Otherwise, if repairs are not made, the marriage will soon deteriorate and become worse. Why not start with you?

However, in certain kinds of marriages, trying harder in this way is not a good idea and can actually make the marriage worse. When I wrote my book *How to Act Right When Your Spouse Acts Wrong,* I was careful to be clear that there is no cookie-cutter approach to being a godly spouse. What would be the right thing to do in one marriage could be the absolute wrong thing to do in another.

Let's look at why in some marriages trying harder to accommodate your husband, to do what he wants and needs, or to be more compliant and submissive to what he demands becomes destructive not only to you, but also to him and to your marriage.

Trying Harder Feeds the Lie

In some marriages, trying harder does not engender a reciprocal response. It has the opposite effect. It feeds the fantasy that the sole purpose of your life is to serve your husband, make him happy, and meet his every need. It feeds his belief of entitlement and his selfishness, and it solidifies his self-deception that it is indeed all about him.

When destructive behaviors are a regular pattern in your marriage, understand this important truth: Your husband doesn't want a real wife who will reflect to him her pain when he hurts her or God's wisdom when she sees him making a foolish decision. What he demands is a fantasy wife, a blow-up punching-bag wife who continues to bounce back with a smile even when he knocks her down. He wants a doll wife who always agrees, always acts nice, always smiles, and thinks he's wonderful all the time, no matter what he does or how he behaves. He wants a wife who loves to have sex with him whenever he's in the mood, regardless of how he treats her. He wants a wife who doesn't ask anything of him or hold him accountable for anything, yet allows him to do whatever he pleases. He wants a wife who will never upset him, never disagree with him, or never challenge him. He wants a wife who grants him amnesty whenever he messes up, never mentioning it again even if the same sin happens again and again. Trying harder to become the fantasy wife is not helpful to your husband or your marriage.

Trying harder to become the fantasy wife is not
helpful to your husband or your marriage.

The more you collude with his idea that he's entitled to a fantasy wife, the more firmly entrenched this lie becomes. You will never measure up to his fantasy wife because you, too, are a sinner. You will fail him (as every partner does in a marriage) and won't always meet his needs (or wants). In addition, you are created by God as your own unique, separate person. Therefore you will have feelings of your own and won't always agree with everything he says or wants. It is not your sole purpose to serve him and meet his every need. Trying to be his fantasy wife not only hurts him, but it hurts you too. It diminishes the person God has made you to be because your husband has now become your god. He dictates who you are to be and what you are to do. And when you bow to this god, you soon become ruled by fear, not God's love. Your spirit becomes deformed, and you will never grow to be the woman God created you to be.

In healthy marriages, individuals must let go of their idea of a fantasy spouse and learn to love the real person they've married. They must learn to handle disagreements, differences, and conflicts with this real person they've married. This comes through compromise, mutual caring, and mutual submission. Sacrifice and service are mutually practiced in order to love each other in godly ways. When we fail (as we will), we see the hurt or pain in our partner's eyes and, with God's help, will make the corrections so that damages are repaired and love grows. In a destructive marriage, when real wife and fantasy wife collide, it is never pretty.

Most women who keep trying harder to please their husbands do so because that's what they believe God expects them to do. God does call you to love and respect your husband and to be your husband's helpmate, but you may be surprised at what that really looks like. Do you think God is asking you to try harder to become your husband's fantasy wife (which you will never succeed at), or does God have you in your husband's life for a far more radical and redemptive purpose?

In her book *Lost Women of the Bible,* Carolyn Custis James points out that the Hebrew word for "helpmate," *ezer,* is "a powerful Hebrew military word whose significance we have barely begun to unpack." She wrote, "The *ezer* is a warrior, and this has far-reaching implications for women, not only in marriage, but in every relationship, season, and walk of life." She continues, "Eve and all her daughters are *ezers*—strong warriors who stand alongside their brothers in the battle for God's kingdom."[1] This means you are going to fight (God's way) to bring about your husband's growth and his good. You are going to allow God to use you to meet your husband's real needs, not just his felt needs.

Stop and ask yourself this question: *What do I think my husband needs the most from me right now?* No cheating. Give yourself a few minutes to really ponder your answer. It's crucial that you learn to think clearly, if you want to make some changes for yourself. Does he need you to continue to prop him up—to indulge his self-centeredness, destructive behaviors, and self-deception? Or does he need something far more risky?

Trust me. Your husband doesn't need you to indulge his fantasy or collude with his internal lie that says he is entitled to the perks of a good marriage while sowing the seeds of destruction and selfishness. What he needs most (for his welfare) is a real wife who is a godly woman. He needs a wife who will love him enough to tell him the truth and to respectfully challenge his selfishness, his self-absorption, and his self-deception. That indeed is risky love and redemptive love, and it's difficult to do with the right heart and actions. It's the laying-down-your-life kind of love because you do not know how he will respond or what will happen to you or your marriage once you do it.

> Your husband doesn't need you to indulge his fantasy
> or collude with his internal lie that says he is entitled
> to the perks of a good marriage while sowing
> the seeds of destruction and selfishness.

You might be feeling scared right now. You're not sure you can (or want to) love your husband in that way. Take a deep breath; we'll work together to learn how to get there. In the next chapters I am going to help you prepare, both internally and strategically, how to love your spouse in this radical new way. But before we do that, let me clear up one more area that has confused both men and women far too long.

Misunderstandings About Biblical Headship and Submission

As a young wife, I attended a retreat that was geared around becoming a godly woman. Most of the wives in the room groaned when they heard the *S* word featured as our next topic. No wife looks forward to hearing that God says she must give her husband the final say in all decisions, regardless of how capable or stable he is, just because he's the man.

Throughout the session the speaker emphasized how God created the husband as the head of the home to be the leader. She said that even if our husbands made poor decisions, God would protect us and our children if we simply trusted Him and obeyed our husbands. Then she proceeded to tell a story where a woman's husband wanted her to have an abortion. The wife didn't want to, but she submitted, and just before she was to go to the clinic for the procedure, she had a spontaneous miscarriage. "See," the speaker said, "God was faithful."

I wanted to stand up and scream "That's crazy. Don't listen to her!" but I was too much of a coward at the time to risk such censure from the group. I'm braver today. I'm telling you, don't fall for that kind of simplistic and naive teaching on this very important subject. If you want to get clearheaded and be a godly woman, in addition to listening to wise counsel, you must study the Scriptures yourself and ask God to help you understand what the Bible says. Jesus tells us that he gives each one of us, as believers, the Holy Spirit, which he promises leads us into all truth (see John 16:13).

The Bible never says that submission is only a wife's or woman's responsibility, nor does it say that the husband or man gets the final say in all decisions. These ideas have been misrepresented and misunderstood. Wrongly applied they can cause harm to men, women, and children, as well as thwart God's plan for loving family relationships.

During a counseling session, Natalie said, "I've always been taught that submission to my husband trumps everything, even my children. But when he's raging out of control, screaming, and threatening them, and their scared little faces look to me for help, what am I supposed to do? Does God want me to support my husband and ignore what's happening because he's the head of our home?"

The New Testament never describes godly headship or leadership by using an example of an authoritarian exercising power over someone. Jesus demonstrated headship for his disciples so that they would be crystal clear about what he meant. Instead of demonstrating his leadership or headship by wielding his mighty power and rightful authority, he donned a towel and basin and personally washed each disciple's dirty feet. They were the future leaders of his church, and Jesus wanted to show them that biblical headship meant sacrificial servanthood. Neither Jesus nor the Scriptures ever describe biblical headship or leadership as entitlement to do what you want, demanding that others do what you want, or permission to get your own way. The correct biblical terms for those characteristics are *selfishness* and *misuse of one's power and authority*. There are numerous examples of these behaviors throughout Scripture, but they are never depicted as God's example of leadership, but rather as sin. (Read through the seven chapters of the Old Testament's book of Micah for numerous examples of leaders abusing their power and God's response.)

After Jesus finished washing his disciples' feet, he said to each of them, "If I then, your Lord and Teacher, have washed your feet, you also ought to wash one another's feet. For I have given you an example, that you also should do just as I have done to you" (John 13:14–15). This concept of selfless servanthood was so radically different from his disciples' idea of leadership that they didn't truly grasp what Jesus meant. Later on, James and John were arguing about who would have the better seat in heaven, when Jesus stopped them and taught them the essence of biblical headship. He said, "You know that those who are considered rulers of the Gentiles lord it over them, and their great ones exercise authority over them. *But it shall not be so among you.* But whoever would be great among you must be your servant, and whoever would be first among you must be slave of all" (Mark 10:42–44). Jesus expressly warned his leaders not to abuse their power just to get their way or to boss people around (see Luke 22:25–26; Matthew 23:3–4).

What Jesus taught was unheard of in Jewish culture. Hierarchy was well established even in the most intimate relationships. Men dominated women, husbands their wives. Paul picked up Jesus's heart on the subject of headship in marriage when he wrote, "Husbands, love your wives, as Christ loved the church and gave himself up for her" (Ephesians 5:25). The essence of biblical teaching on headship is that if you are the leader, your responsibility is to initiate and model servanthood before anyone else in the family does. As the leader, you're to show the way. You're to go first. When a leader (whether of a home, a church, or a nation) manipulates, threatens, or scares people into doing what he says or to get what he wants, know that he is not behaving as a biblical head, but rather as a bully.[2] As Paul wrote, "Husbands, love your wives and never treat them harshly" (Colossians 3:19, NLT), and he describes love by saying, "It does not demand its own way" (1 Corinthians 13:5, NLT).

Jesus didn't only model headship for us; he also modeled submission. In the Garden of Gethsemane, anticipating the crucifixion, Jesus prayed that this cup of suffering would be removed from him. He dreaded the cross; he wanted God to find an alternate way to save humankind. Yet, Jesus submitted himself when he prayed, "Nevertheless, not my will, but yours, be done" (Luke 22:42). Throughout his life, Jesus always wanted to do what God wanted. He said his will was synonymous with God's will (see John 4:34; 6:38; 5:30; 8:29; 12:49–50). Now in this agonizing moment during his garden prayer, Jesus felt differently. This was the first time he didn't want to do what God wanted, but he chose submission to God's will and his Father's perfect plan. God didn't force Jesus to submit; Jesus chose to. Jesus said, "No one takes it from me, but I lay it down of my own accord" (10:18).

In the same way, biblical submission can never be forced. It can only be done by the one who chooses to submit her (or his) will to another. When we voluntarily give our will to another or to God, it's called submission; when someone forces our will to be given, it is not biblical submission. The correct terms are *intimidation, coercion,* and *bullying.* Submission isn't necessarily agreement; it's yielding your will to another for a greater good. The good might be unity in the family (or body of Christ) or honoring and pleasing God.

The apostle Paul wrote in Philippians that we must be intentional if we don't want selfishness to rule in our relationships (see Philippians 2:2–4). He then used Christ's example for us to see how that works. Paul wrote, "Have this mind among yourselves, which is yours in Christ Jesus, who, though he was in the form of God, did not count equality with God a thing to be grasped, but emptied himself, by taking the form of a servant, being born in the likeness of men. And being found in human form, he humbled himself by becoming obedient to the point of death, even death on a cross" (Philippians 2:5–8).

Jesus modeled both headship and submission in volunteering for the servant's place and yielding his will to God. This describes the working together of headship and submission; the husband sacrificially leads his wife in servanthood (through example), and the wife sacrificially yields her will in servanthood (through example). Both are servants of the other and of God. When only one is the servant or the other is the master or god, the marriage isn't working as God intended.

Since the fall of Adam and Eve, human beings have been vying for power and control over one another (see Genesis 3:16). This was not God's original plan, but rather the result of sin. Biblical headship doesn't mean you get your way all the time, and submission doesn't mean you have no voice or choice in the matter. The Scriptures validate the mutuality of marriage and the dignity and value of each individual, no matter who they are. As Paul plainly wrote, there is no difference between Jew and Gentile, slave and free, man or woman (see Galatians 3:28). We may have different roles and responsibilities, but one is not over the other. Mutuality of servanthood, submission, and sacrifice is the biblical model for the Trinity and for godly relationships, including marriage.

Now that your eyes have been opened and you see more clearly, you may be tempted to go in one of two directions. The first one we've already mentioned. You're too terrified to do anything different than you've always done because you know that doing so will cause upheaval and you're afraid of the unknown. You want to close this book right now and throw it under the bed or in the trash. You don't want to know more. Please don't do that. Your safety, your children's future, and your husband's well-being depend on you moving forward in a new way.

The other direction is to start attacking your spouse with your newfound awareness and both guns blazing. If you do that, you may get his attention, but you will not win his heart or have the opportunity to impact the way he thinks. Rather, he will run for cover and think you've lost your mind.

Instead, calm your heart down. You don't have to do anything different in your marriage just yet, but I do want you to do a few things for yourself. First, finish reading the rest of this book so you will grow and gain more wisdom and strategies on what to do when you're ready. At some point you will need to have a conversation with your husband, but first let's make sure you are prepared to do it well.

Second, I hope you've already been talking with God, but if not, start now. Humbly ask God to show you what your husband needs from you and how to best love your husband biblically. Don't worry right now if you don't think you can do it, but do ask God to give you wisdom to know how to love your husband and for the courage to do it when the time is right.

One of my coaching clients recently told me, "I've finally understood that loving my husband biblically doesn't mean I keep enduring and forbearing his pornography and extramarital affairs. It means I say, 'No more.'"

This year I read the story of Louie Zamperini in *Unbroken: A World War II Story of Survival, Resilience, and Redemption* by Laura Hillenbrand. Louie Zamperini was an Olympic-bound runner who was captured during World War II by the Japanese and held as a prisoner of war for years. His story of survival is incredible, but it was the attitudes and behaviors of the prison guards that grabbed my attention. As they systematically humiliated and abused their prisoners, they also dehumanized and degraded themselves. Sin and abuse is destructive to our personhood, whether we are the victims or the perpetrators.

Change begins with you, if you no longer want to be in a destructive marriage. Simply trying harder to be the perfect fantasy wife will not help. It only feeds the selfish monster (which we all have) and allows it to grow unchallenged. That is not good for your husband, your marriage, your children, or for you. For the best interests of everyone in your family, it's time to initiate some changes.

Dear God,

I am tired of trying to be the fantasy wife. I have failed. I don't know how to be a true biblical helpmate to my husband. It feels scary. God help me not to retaliate with my new awareness. Help me not to throw things in my husband's face that he's gotten wrong all these years. But as you are teaching me and changing me, please be working in his heart too.

Action Step: What are your husband's greatest-felt needs (for example: control, sex, unchallenged respect, affirmation)? What do you think his real needs are (for example: humility, repentance, self-awareness, wisdom, truth, forgiveness)?

What is one thing you could do or say this week to meet one of your husband's real needs?

Seven

Build Your Core

See that no one renders evil for evil to anyone, but always pursue what is good both for yourselves and for all.

—1 Thessalonians 5:15, NKJV

My friend Barb's beach house is a little slice of heaven on earth. Her home away from home is built right on the boardwalk, and I can sit on her balcony and watch children fly kites and dolphins play. I love the salty air, the ocean breezes, and all the foods I don't normally eat—like extra cheesy Manco & Manco pizza and lemon Polish Water Ice. Barb and I get up early in the morning before it gets too hot and take our power walk up one end of the boardwalk and down the other. The last morning of our minivacation was exceptionally hot, and ten minutes into our walk, I was already drenched in salty, sticky sweat, my hair matted close to my head. When we completed our five-mile trek, Barb turned toward me, her hair still fluffy with her skin only slightly glistening, and said, "Leslie, I've noticed you've been slouching."

Slouching? Really? In this heat, what do you expect? I thought to myself. Barb's words stung hard, but I knew she was right. I had exercised most of my adult life, but over the past few years, admittedly, I had gotten lazy, and I guess it showed more than I noticed, not only in my waistline but in my posture. When I returned home, I called a gym and made an appointment with someone who could help me.

The following week I reluctantly met with Chris, a young, burly fitness trainer who pushed me through a battery of tests and finished our evaluation by whipping out a camera. Already I felt old, frumpy, and fat…but it got worse. You know the saying, "A picture doesn't lie"? The truth was right in front of me. My shoulders slumped, my belly pouched out, my back swayed, and my neck and chin somehow jutted out from my shoulders in a most unflattering way—and I had worked hard to stand up straight when he took the picture. Chris turned to me, eyebrows raised, and said, "You need to build your core."

"What's that?" I asked, dreading his response.

"Your core muscles wrap around your abdomen and back, and they support your spine and keep you balanced and stable," Chris said. "Bottom line, a strong core keeps you from slouching and looking old." Then he asked, "Are you ready to get to work?"

"Um, let me think about this for a few days," I stammered, anxious to bolt out of there as soon as possible.

After a good cry, I realized I was faced with a tough choice. I was either going to work hard to strengthen my core muscles, or I could continue to do nothing and become fatter and more slouched. I didn't like those two alternatives. I wanted Chris to tell me that there was a third choice—a pill I could take, a massage I could get, something that didn't hurt and was easier than working out with weights three times a week. But that wasn't one of my options if I wanted to improve my core, my weight, and my overall body alignment. If I wanted change, I would need to invest my time, my energy, and—if I wanted Chris's help—my money to strengthen my core.

Core strength isn't only necessary for our physical bodies. We need core strength to support our mental, spiritual, and emotional health as well. Right about now you realize that you have some difficult choices in front of you. Believe me, I know change is hard, and sometimes we're only motivated to change when the pain of staying the same becomes greater than the fear or pain of making the change. You can choose to grow stronger through this destructive marriage or not, but if you choose to do nothing, you need to understand what it will cost you: your emotional, mental, and spiritual core will get weaker and weaker, curving inward until your entire personhood is out of alignment. Sacrificing yourself by allowing someone to sin against you to keep peace in your marriage is never a wise choice—not for you, not for your husband, not for your marriage. God calls us to be biblical peacemakers, not peacekeepers or peace fakers.

> Change is hard, and sometimes we're only motivated to change when the pain of staying the same becomes greater than the fear or pain of making the change.

In my counseling and coaching practice, I've taken to heart Jeremiah's warning to the prophets of Israel when he scolded them for putting Band-Aids on serious problems. He told them, "You heal the wounds of my people superficially by saying 'peace, peace' when there is no peace" (see Jeremiah 6:14). Pretending or keeping up appearances for the sake of staying married won't bring healing to serious marital wounds any more than a Band-Aid can stop arterial bleeding. And pretending and peacekeeping isn't what God calls us to anyway. Biblical peacemaking involves being prepared to enter into battle in order to bring about the possibility for true shalom peace, reconciliation, and restoration of your marriage. If you want to become God's *ezer* (strong warrior) so that you'll be prepared to fight for your husband's well-being and your marital future, you first need to strengthen your core.

> God calls us to be biblical peacemakers,
> not peacekeepers or peace fakers.

Whether you're in a destructive marriage or not, these four core strengths are essential to build and maintain good mental, emotional, spiritual, and relational health. I will use the acronym CORE to help you remember what they are. With God at the center and with his help, I will choose to be:

Committed to truth and reality

Open to growth, instruction, and feedback

Responsible for myself and Respectful toward others without dishonoring myself

Empathic and compassionate toward others without enabling people to continue to abuse and disrespect me

We will explore each of these four CORE strengths in detail below. And in the following chapters, I'm going to show you how they help you grow stronger and give you the wisdom to handle a destructive spouse.

CORE Strength 1: <u>Committed</u> to Truth and Reality

"I can't breathe," Maggie sobbed, her eyes swollen and rimmed in red. "I don't know what to do. I can't sleep. I can't work. I can't eat. I'm a mess."

I nodded. It was hard to ignore Maggie's body rebelling over a recent decision she had made to reconcile with her husband, Brad. Eighteen months earlier, Maggie separated from him due to his womanizing. She had endured years of verbal abuse, selfishness, and extreme control, but learning of his affairs with other women pushed her over the edge. She left their marriage, hoping and praying that he'd come to his senses. Instead, Brad filed for divorce.

Maggie hated being divorced. She knew she was getting older and didn't look like she used to, and she feared that she'd be alone for the rest of her life. Almost a year later Brad called her, asking her if they could reconcile their marriage.

After Brad's call, Maggie came to see me. She was beaming. "Brad told me he is going to church. He is done with other women. He is different now," Maggie said. "He wants to get back together. What do you think?"

Since their divorce, Maggie hadn't let go of her dream that God would bring Brad to his senses and he would come back to her. After his call, she spent hours fantasizing about having a godly husband, a loving marriage, and a great family life.

"What's the rush?" I asked, inviting Maggie to give herself more time. "Why don't you and Brad take it slow and just date for a while. That way you'll be able to see if he's changed."

"He'll never go along with that," Maggie said. "He said the Bible says God hates divorce, and he wants us to get back together as soon as possible."

"But, Maggie," I cautioned, "what if he hasn't changed?"

Maggie wouldn't hear me. She was anxious to live out her fantasy dream marriage, and so she capitulated to Brad's charm. Now, four weeks later, she was back in my office, curled up on my couch, barely able to catch her breath.

"Maggie, you're trembling," I said. "What do you think your body is trying to tell you right now?"

Her voice cracked. "I think it's telling me Brad isn't any different, and I've made a terrible mistake. I'm so scared."

Maggie wanted to believe her ex-husband had changed into the loving, patient, unselfish, and faithful husband she always longed for. When she tentatively expressed some of her ambivalent feelings around their rapid reconciliation, the signs of disrespect, controlling abuse, and selfishness quickly reared their ugly heads. Brad told Maggie she was being ridiculous. They were wasting time and money in two separate households. If she wanted to reconcile, she would need to submit to his decisions. As always, Maggie did what Brad wanted, but her body didn't like it one bit.

As Maggie learned the hard way, one of the best predictors of future behavior is past behavior. If a man tells you he's changed, don't automatically believe him until you observe his actions and attitudes over time. I'll talk more in chapters 12 and 13 about specific changes we're looking for that make a destructive marriage more likely to heal, but for now I want you to concentrate on this one important truth: *It is not your husband's lies that will do the most damage to you. It's the lies you tell yourself.*

> It is not your husband's lies that will do the most damage to you. It's the lies you tell yourself.

All of us are prone to self-deception—no exceptions. Maggie preferred her version of reality because it made her feel hopeful and happy, though she saw no evidence of change in her ex-husband's character or in his habits. The Bible tells us, "He [or she] feeds on ashes, a deluded heart misleads him; he cannot save himself, or say, 'Is not this thing in my right hand a lie?'" (Isaiah 44:20, NIV). In this passage, the writer is referring to people who carved wooden idols for themselves and then treated the idols as gods. He challenged them with, *How crazy is that?* Yet in the same way, Maggie's craving for a loving marriage and godly husband blinded her to what was happening right in front of her own nose.

As CORE strength number one reminds us, if you want to grow to be strong and wise, you must have a commitment not only to external truth, but to internal truth. The psalmist prayed, "Behold, you delight in truth in the inward being, and you teach me wisdom in the secret heart" (Psalm 51:6). If you're going to stop pretending, placating, avoiding reality, and living in fantasy land, you need to face the truth—not only about your marriage and your spouse, but also about yourself.

Maggie wasn't quite ready to face the truth about Brad, but her body forced her to acknowledge the truth about her own limitations. Her body refused to lie to her. It refused to cooperate with her fantasy that everything was fine. Maggie managed a smile on the outside, but her insides felt like a category-five hurricane, shaking her up until she paid attention. When Maggie saw that she could not function, she wired up her courage and told Brad that she wasn't ready to fully reconcile with him yet; she needed more time. He could see she was a mess, but when she told him she had to move out again, he got angry and tried to bully her to back down; but Maggie stayed centered on the truth. Maggie also began to take a hard look at how dependent she'd been on Brad their entire marriage, which kept her immature and unprepared to function as an adult outside the marriage. To get healthier and stronger as a person, Maggie knew that she needed to make some changes and was now ready to do the hard work of not only truth seeking and truth telling, but also truth doing (see John 3:21).

The interesting thing is that once Maggie stood up for herself and told the truth about her inability to rush their reconciliation, Brad backed down and agreed to go to counseling to get help to put their relationship back together. Time will tell, but that was a healthy step toward positive change.

CORE Strength 2: Open to Growth, Instruction, and Feedback

Not long ago I was speaking with my brother who owns a large business in downtown Chicago. He said, "Leslie, I can't believe the number of highly intelligent people who have zero self-awareness. They have no idea how they come across, and surprisingly they're unwilling to be told or taught."

Please don't let that be you. We're all broken and sinful, but not everyone can see it or will admit it. The Bible calls it blindness, and it is our biggest impediment to healing destructive relationships, especially a marriage. When we think we know everything and aren't open to learning or changing, the Bible calls us fools, no matter how smart we are or how many degrees we have after our names. Jesus called the religious leaders of his day hypocrites and blind guides because they were not open to recognizing their pride or seeing themselves as sinful men in need of a Savior (see Matthew 15:14; Matthew 23:24). As a result, they never changed. Instead, they focused all their energy on getting rid of him. They hated hearing the truth.

One of the scariest things you must do if you want to become whole is to be honest with yourself and admit you need help. This isn't only true for your destructive husband; it's true for you as well. Once you are honest with yourself about your sin problem and your blindness, then there is hope for a solution. Trust me, no one becomes a healthy individual without the willingness to hear feedback and receive correction from God, the Scriptures, as well as other wise people. But that willingness requires humility.

Humility means we agree to lower ourselves and acknowledge we can't do it all by ourselves. We need help to change. The psalmist prayed, "Teach me your way, O Lord, and lead me on a level path because of my enemies" (Psalm 27:11). It is precisely when dealing with an enemy that we need the most help. Otherwise, in our humanness we will naturally respond poorly. We get resentful, we retaliate, we seek revenge, and often we return evil for evil. Some of us believe the lie that everything wrong in our marriage is entirely our husband's fault and that we are sinless victims. Others believe the lie that if only we could figure out what to do differently, our husband would change and become the man we've always dreamed of.

To be taught, you must be willing to see the truth; and in order to grow in truth, you must be open to learning new things from God and other wise people (see Psalm 25). The Bible tells us that we are to be teachable, and that means not just learning what ways are true, good, and right, but actually doing them (see James 1:22–25). Be careful who you listen to. There are some individuals who are biblically literate but spiritually foolish. Don't be deceived into thinking someone is wise just because she speaks spiritual-sounding words, if her attitudes and actions consistently don't match up.

I've been working with a coaching client who has gained strength because her heart is eager to grow in God's ways and learn new things. She said, "Leslie, my parents never taught me how to apply Scripture to my life. I was thrown into the deep end of the pool of life, and I had to either sink or swim. I didn't sink, but I never really learned to swim either; I just survived. I have no idea how to respond when my husband acts like a jerk. My default reaction is that I'm quietly resentful and I simmer until I blow up and become sharp and shaming. Help me do better."

I love that she is so aware and honest with herself. I love that she wants to grow and learn how to handle things within her marriage in a godly way.

CORE Strength 3: <u>Responsible</u> for Myself and <u>Respectful</u> Toward Others Without Dishonoring Myself

When we live with a difficult and/or destructive person, it takes its toll on us. Over and over we get hurt, angry, worn out, and afraid. If we are not extremely careful, it's quite likely that we will start to become destructive too. Why? Because serious sin not only affects us, it infects us with its poison. If we don't guard our hearts, we can become like the very thing we hate.

Julia and David were in full-time Christian ministry. Over the years Julia sought some advice from me about how to deal with David's critical and overbearing personality, but being in ministry made it very scary to be honest with other people. She feared if she told the truth about their marriage, they might lose their jobs and suffer financially. But things got so bad that Julia refused to pretend anymore, and finally their ministry leaders mandated them into counseling.

She and David were now sitting in my office. I had expected David to be defensive and argumentative, but I was surprised to observe a humble openness. Their marital crisis and accountability to their ministry leaders appeared to have softened him. He admitted he needed help— something that he had never been willing to do before. I thought Julia would be ecstatic that her husband was finally open to counseling and changing.

"I've been a terrible husband," he said. "I want to learn how to be more sensitive to Julia, but I know I'm not going to change overnight. This past weekend, I thought everything was going great. We had a wonderful evening. We went to dinner, and then we went to a furniture store to look at a new bed. I found one that she said she liked, and I bought it for her. I want her to be happy."

Julia sat like a stone, her face turned toward the door. While David was talking, I noticed she rolled her eyes and pursed her lips. I asked Julia how she felt the weekend went.

"It wasn't as great as David thinks," she said. "I told him I didn't want to go look for a different bed, but of course he didn't hear me—as usual. Don't get me wrong, I loved the bed. But that's not the point. I didn't want him to buy it. I don't even know if we're going to stay married, so why in the world would I want to get a new bed together?"

Once again David's controlling personality overruled Julia's no, and she was furious. In trying to do something nice for his wife, he still behaved insensitively to her stated feelings and boundaries. Their counseling session ended, but I asked Julia to stay behind for a few minutes longer.

I said, "What's happening to you, Julia?"

Julia softened. "I hate how I'm feeling," she said. "When I try to speak up and say no to him, he never hears me. If I'm nice to him for a minute, he thinks everything is better, and it's not. I feel furious and so resentful."

"I see that," I said. "You have every reason to be angry, but in your anger and frustration, you're losing sight of your CORE strengths, especially the third one, 'I will be responsible for myself and respectful toward others without dishonoring myself.'"

Julia agreed and began to work more intentionally on what she needed to do differently when David was overbearing or not listening to her. She didn't know what was going to happen with their marriage, but she wanted to make sure she didn't disrespect her husband or dishonor herself in the way she responded.

I'm going to make a huge assumption right now—and I may be wrong for some of you. I think you are reading this book because you want your marriage to be different. Like Julia, you want your husband to get it and to change. I want to help you toward that end, but I guarantee it won't happen if you are overcome with your husband's sin against you and let it infect you with resentment. One of the phrases I always use with those I'm coaching or counseling is this: *If you are going to stay in this marriage, then stay well; and if you are going to leave your marriage, then leave well.* In other words, you are responsible for the person you are and are becoming in the fire of this difficult marriage. It is important to realize that you give God no glory, nor do your children any favors, if you stay married with a heart full of bitterness, resentment, fear, hatred, or indifference. God wants much more for you than that.

You give God no glory, nor do your children any favors, if you stay married with a heart full of bitterness, resentment, fear, hatred, or indifference. God wants much more for you than that.

Therefore, our third core strength—taking responsibility for ourselves and being respectful—means that we must choose to guard our hearts so that we are not overcome with evil. Once we recognize that we have been infected with evil's poison or are spewing out some of our own, we must take care of ourselves—or get help—so that resentment, indifference, and our human tendency to pay evil back with more evil of our own does not become part of our character. We commit to treat our husbands with respect even when they don't deserve it, because we understand how we treat people is much more a statement about who we are rather than how they act. In the same way, how your husband treats you is not about you; it says something about who he is.

When you choose to treat people with respect because that's the person you want to be, you will gain self-respect, which enables you to respond wisely when your husband doesn't treat you well.

CORE STRENGTH 4: <u>EMPATHIC</u> AND COMPASSIONATE TOWARD OTHERS WITHOUT ENABLING PEOPLE TO CONTINUE TO ABUSE OR DISRESPECT ME

We can't help but feel angry and hurt when we are mistreated, but, as we've seen, those emotions can quickly harden into bitterness and resentment if we're not vigilant. It's crucial that you not lose your empathy and compassion even in a destructive marriage.

The capacity for empathy and compassion is hard wired by God into the human heart and brain. It is essential for all relationships to be maintained and healed. Jesus tells us that we are to treat people as we would want to be treated, not as they deserve (see Luke 6:31). Perhaps one of the reasons your husband behaves the way he does—with no remorse or change—is he has lost his ability to feel your pain or is incapable of genuine empathy and compassion for others.

If that's the case, do you want to be like that? When we lose empathy and compassion for others, or never had it, our darker selfish sides will always rule, and we cannot maintain loving connections with others. Whenever we behave as our worst selves, we do not and cannot feel good about ourselves.

> When we lose our empathy and compassion for others,
> or never had it, our darker selfish sides will always rule.

One of the things that kills empathy and compassion for someone we once felt love toward is the buildup of negative emotions, especially resentment. Jesus knows that when we're struggling with the effects of a person's sin against us, we will feel angry, scared, and hurt. That is human and normal. But when the person who has hurt us is not sorry, or continues to hurt us again and again, our negative emotions grow and resentment builds, putting a choke hold on all our positive feelings. I believe that is one reason why the Bible commands us to forgive when someone hurts us and why Jesus tells us to love our enemy by doing him or her good. It's not only for their benefit but for ours, so that we don't fill up with resentment and become toxic.

Doing good toward your enemy may not make any difference to

him, but it will make a huge difference in you. It's not what your husband does to you that will do the most damage to your personhood, but rather what you do with what he does to you. Do you allow it to destroy you? Do you allow it to embitter you? Do you allow its poison to suck all the goodness and love from your soul so that all that's left is a shriveled-up heart that snarls and shames and scoots to safety in order to not get hurt again?

> It's not what your husband does to you that will
> do the most damage to your personhood,
> but rather what you do with what he does to you.

It sounds crazy, contrary to what we would humanly think of as a smart thing to do, but ask God to give you his heart of compassion for your spouse. Empathy for your husband does not mean enabling him or trusting him or allowing him to hurt you. It means you recognize he's a sinner just like you. You feel sad for the man he has become instead of mad that he is such a lousy husband. It means you will not treat him as he deserves, but you will treat him as a human being who is created in God's image. (In chapters 9 and 10, I'll show you how to communicate hard truth without using contempt, shame, or disrespect, which will give you a much better chance at being heard.)

I want you to know that even if you feel helpless or powerless in your marriage, you do have choices. You can choose to grow in Christlike character through your difficult circumstances, or you can succumb to the lies of your real enemy, Satan. The Bible warns us, "Be self-controlled and alert. Your enemy the devil prowls around like a roaring lion looking for someone to devour" (1 Peter 5:8, NIV). The devil may already be chomping away at your husband's heart, but don't let him get yours too. Maintaining your empathy and compassion not only protects you from staying a victim, but it protects you from becoming an abuser.

Marital adversity not only reveals character; it shapes it. You have a choice about how that shaping is taking place right now. When you know and believe that you are a loveable, valuable, worthwhile human being and live from that core place, then toxic people lose their power to manipulate you. They can't control and intimidate you as they once did when you felt worthless, dependent, and needy. If you don't strengthen your core, you will always live from your circumstances and your emotions. On the other hand, when you live from your core, your abusive/destructive husband might permanently damage your marriage, but he cannot destroy you.

Remember, to build CORE strength you must commit to truth. Refuse to pretend. Learn all you can, and be open to God and wise people to teach you and encourage you in the way forward. Take responsibility for your own behaviors and responses when your husband is acting destructively. He may dishonor you, but don't dishonor yourself. Finally, deal with your own building resentment and bitterness so that you maintain your empathy and compassion. Empathy is not the same as enabling someone to continue their destructive behaviors toward you. You can compassionately say no, or call the police if needed.

Your CORE reflects who you are as well as who you want to be.

Dear God,

I need CORE strength. I feel weak and shriveled and bent over. My internal posture is out of alignment, and I need help in getting stronger. I don't want to allow my husband's behavior to determine the person I am going to be. Please help me work on these four steps and give me someone who will walk alongside of me.

Action Step: Memorize the four components to CORE, and pick one of the four to intentionally practice this week. Consider the difference between *empathy* and *feeling compelled to take responsibility to fix someone else's problem.* Start by reading Galatians 6:2–4. Where have you been carrying the responsibility for your husband when he should be caring his own load?

Eight

Get Prepared to Confront Wisely

If another believer sins against you, go
privately and point out the offense. If
the other person listens and confesses it,
you have won that person back. But if you
are unsuccessful, take one or two others
with you and go back again, so that everything you say may be confirmed by two or
three witnesses. If the person still refuses
to listen, take your case to the church.
Then if he or she won't accept the church's
decision, treat that person as a pagan or
a corrupt tax collector.

—Jesus, in Matthew 18:15–17, NLT

Sharon was working on building her CORE but wasn't fully comfortable when we started talking about what she needed to do next.
She said, "I'm sure our marriage is emotionally destructive based on all
I've read and everything you said, but I am as much a sinner as my husband is. I am no more deserving of grace than he is."

"You're right, Sharon," I said, curious as to where this was going.

She continued. "The Bible teaches that love covers a multitude of sins [see 1 Peter 4:8]. And it is good to overlook an offense [see Proverbs 19:11]. As I think about that powerful gospel truth, I wonder, is it right of me to confront my husband at all? Shouldn't I just keep quiet and minister to him, and pray that he will see God's love in me?"

Some of you might be wondering the same thing. Jesus makes it clear. It is not our right or responsibility to judge or condemn anyone (see Matthew 7:1–2). God does instruct believers to forbear with and forgive one another, and Jesus reminds us to take the log out of our own eye before we attempt to remove the speck in someone else's eye (see Matthew 7:3–5). To bring up every offense that occurs in our marriage would become tiresome indeed.

I told Sharon that love does cover a multitude of sins but not all sins. The Bible also instructs us to warn those who are lazy (see 1 Thessalonians 5:14). We are not to participate in unfruitful deeds of darkness (see Ephesians 5:11). We're told to bring a brother back who has wandered from the truth (see James 5:19), as well as restore someone who is caught in a trespass (see Galatians 6:1). When someone deeply offends us, Jesus tells us that we're to go talk with him. Not so that we can tell him off or condemn him, but so that our relationship can be repaired and restored (see Matthew 18:15–17).[1]

"Yes," I told Sharon, "the Bible teaches us that we ought to forgive and forbear, overlooking minor offenses, hoping others will do the same for us. And we are to speak up when someone's sin is hurting them, hurting others, or hurting us."

Serious and repetitive sin is lethal to any relationship. We would not be loving our husbands or doing them good if we kept quiet and colluded with their self-deception or enabled their sin to flourish without any attempt to speak truth into their lives (see Ephesians 4:15). Yes, we are called to be imitators of Christ and live a life of love; however, let's be careful that we do not put a heavy burden on ourselves (or allow someone else to put it on us) to do something that God himself does not do. God is gracious and compassionate to the saint and unrepentant sinner alike, but he does not have a close relationship with both. He says our sins separate us from him (see Isaiah 59:2; Jeremiah 5:25).

When someone repeatedly and seriously sins against us and is not willing to look at what he's done and is not willing to change, it is not possible to have a warm or close or healthy relationship. Loving someone unconditionally is not synonymous with having an unconditional relationship with him. There is an important distinction. God says he loves us unconditionally (see Romans 5:8; 8:38–39), yet God does not have intimate fellowship with the person who will not see his sin and ask for his forgiveness.[2] Jesus's conversations with the Pharisees regularly challenged their self-deception and pride. He did that so they would humble themselves, realize they were wrong, and be able to experience true fellowship with him (see Matthew 23). He loved the religious leaders unconditionally, but they did not enjoy a loving or close relationship. Jesus never pretended otherwise.

A marriage that has no boundaries or conditions is not psychologically healthy, nor is it spiritually sound. It enables your spouse to believe that the normal rules of life don't apply to him, and if he does something hurtful or sinful, he shouldn't have to suffer the consequences of relational fallout. That thinking is not biblical, healthy, or true. For the good of your spouse, your marriage, yourself, and your children, there are times you must make some tough choices. You must speak up, set boundaries, and when necessary implement consequences when your husband's behavior is destroying what God holds so precious—people, marriage, and family. Scripture warns, "He who conceals his sins does not prosper" (Proverbs 28:13, NIV).

"Yes," I said to Sharon. "Your husband desperately needs to see God's love, but he also desperately needs to see himself more truthfully so that he can wake up and ask God to help him make needed changes. You are not better, and God doesn't love you more than your husband. The problem is that your husband has been unwilling to admit to his part of the destruction. He's been unwilling to confess or take responsibility or get the help he needs to change his destructive ways. Instead, he's minimized, denied, lied, excused, rationalized, or blamed others—mostly you."

Confronting someone and/or implementing consequences should never be done as a first step to get someone to hear us, nor is it to be used to scold, shame, condemn, or punish. We have one purpose—to jolt someone awake. We hope that by doing so, he will come to his senses, turn to God, and stop his destructive behaviors.

GET READY, TOUGH CHALLENGES AHEAD

Before you have any direct conversation with your husband about his destructive attitudes or actions, it's important to do some preliminary work so that you are well prepared.

Make Sure You've Developed a Safety Plan

One mark of a healthy woman is she doesn't allow herself to be a repeat victim, if she can help it. If you haven't done so yet, you must develop a safety plan before you have this difficult discussion with your spouse. I hope as you've been working on your CORE strengths, your husband has noticed that something is different about you. You seem stronger, clearer, and wiser. You're not as easily intimidated, nor are you as dependent as you once were. You are not retaliating. You are not reacting as much. You're not begging or pleading. You're not pretending. You're not trying harder to do everything he wants you to do. You are not trying to fix him, and you no longer cover for him or make excuses. You've begun to change.

However, you must be mindful that your husband could get worse before he's willing to get better. Therefore, you need to know how to avoid or get out of an escalating situation and plan for you and your children's safety if you fear he will lose control and try to hurt you.

Document

If you haven't been doing this yet, start now. Jesus says that when you have told someone that his behaviors have hurt you and he refuses to listen, bring other witnesses (see Matthew 18:15–17). In destructive marriages, there often aren't any eyewitnesses, but there can be witness in the form of documentation.

Write down when and where he berates you, what words he uses to demean you, what actions he does that scare you, or what specifically he's done that has left you feeling abandoned. For example, Kristy began documenting dates and details of her husband's indifference. She woke up one night writhing with abdominal pain. She asked her husband to take her to the emergency room. He rolled over and told her to wait until morning. On another occasion Kristy was working outside in her garden, and Bill was heading out to play softball just as Kristy accidently walked into a beehive. Thousands of bees swarmed her, and she screamed for help. Bill got in his car and drove away, laughing at Kristy flailing up and down the front walkway, trying to escape getting stung. She began to swell and had to drive herself to the doctor. When Bill got home, he never asked her how she was, although her face was obviously puffy.

If you have financial records or other bills or receipts that need to be copied to prove deceitful or illegal behaviors, make copies of them. Karla lived in a beautiful multimillion-dollar home. Her husband owned his own business and made plenty of money. Yet he made Karla live off a meager allowance, and he refused to pay for some of her bills. Collect evidence of these facts. Do the same with phone records, tax records, or other papers that demonstrate indifference to your needs or the imbalance of power and control we talked about in chapters 3 and 4. If your husband destroys your property, take pictures or videos that show the damage.

Judy struggled to convince her pastor of her husband's emotional abuse. Her pastor said, "He's such a great guy I can hardly believe what you're telling me, Judy." One Friday evening, while she and her husband were heading home from dinner, they had a mild argument. Fred started raging at Judy, screaming obscenities, swerving in and out of traffic like a madman. Judy pressed her cell phone record button. A few months later, things at home were deteriorating and she approached her pastor a second time for help. This time she was able to play the recording and show photos of three holes Fred had made in the walls of their home during his rages. It was the evidence she needed that added credibility to what she was saying. She was in danger and needed help.

If you or your children are injured because of your husband's behavior, call the police. Go to the emergency room or your family doctor, even if the injuries don't seem to warrant medical attention. You want them documented by a professional and photographs taken, dated, and made part of your medical record. If you feel frightened because he's raging around the house, throwing things, putting his fists through walls, busting doors down—or he threatens to harm you, himself, the children, or your pets—immediately call 911. All you need to say is, "I feel scared of my husband," and tell them what he's doing. You don't have to wait until after something terrible happens to ask for help.

When you document specific incidents and expose what's happening to other witnesses (police, medical personnel, neighbors, church leaders), your husband is less able to lie to himself that his behaviors are not destructive, not illegal, and don't have serious consequences. Documenting also makes you more credible when you ask for support from your church or file for a protection from abuse order from the court. Sometimes when a woman begins to cry out for help, people struggle to believe her story because for the past twenty years, no one suspected a thing. Even her own parents or siblings thought everything was fine. It was never fine, but she worked so hard to make it look that way she has no concrete evidence that it wasn't.

Ask for Support

Getting healthy includes having a group of godly and wise people who will pray for you, support you, and encourage you. That means you will need to be honest with people outside the home about what's going on. Remember, no more pretending. No more covering up. No more making it look as though your family has it all together, when the truth is your marriage is seriously broken.

Sometimes women are told, "[Love] keeps no record of wrongs" (1 Corinthians 13:5, NIV). They feel guilty documenting these problems and exposing their spouses' behaviors to get support from others. This verse doesn't tell you to forget about what happens. That could be very dangerous. This verse tells you not to keep score. Not to allow your anger and hurt to harden your heart with resentment and bitterness that make you feel entitled to retaliate. Your husband will need support and accountability too, if he's willing to make some changes. It's smart to have people who know what's going on and can provide that support when the time comes.

This isn't an opportunity for you to spill the dirt on who your husband is and what he's done to everyone you know. However, once he knows that you will no longer pretend or cover for his behaviors, his power over you diminishes. Once he knows you will no longer allow him to isolate you from a supportive community of people, his ability to intimidate you weakens. Once he knows that you will no longer live the same way you've been living, he may begin to see that he has some tough choices to make, if he wants his marriage to survive.

I would love to tell you to run to your pastor and church leadership for this kind of help, but, sadly, many women I've talked with have found conservative Christian churches give more support to their husbands than to them. Sometimes it's the idea of headship and submission that causes leadership to be wary of a woman who decides she must stand up against what's happening at home. She's seen as contentious, unruly, and lacking a gentle and quiet spirit; therefore, what she reports in her home is seen with suspicion or dismissed. Sometimes it's because her husband is a good liar and manipulator and has charmed the folks at church. He easily makes people believe he's the real victim of abuse, or his wife is exaggerating, lying, or just plain nuts. The last reason I find that pastors don't believe a woman is that by the time she finally reaches the end of her rope, she can't take it anymore. She's so fragile that she's seen as an emotional wreck. Or she's so angry, reactive, bitter, and unforgiving that she's seen as the provoker and cause of their marital problems. Either way, in these types of situations, her side of the story is suspect and her credibility is diminished.

If you do approach your pastor and church family for help, and I hope you do, go prepared with facts, not feelings. For example, Laurie decided to ask her pastor and church leadership for help confronting her husband, Ryan. She went to her appointment armed with specific documentation of his abuse, suspected infidelity, and financial deceit. She told them she needed their support because after many conversations with her husband, he continued to lie to her and to himself. She showed her pastor credit card receipts of charges to unsavory massage parlors and gave him a printout of their cell phone bill that showed Ryan had over four hundred texts in one month to a specific phone number, a woman Ryan met over the Internet. Laurie also was careful not to use the vague term of emotional abuse, but told her pastor the specific words Ryan called her when she confronted him on these issues or whenever he was angry.

Laurie's pastor became deeply troubled when he heard the harshness and vulgar words that Ryan used with his wife. It was difficult for him to believe all that Laurie said, but the evidence she brought was clear. Ryan led a double life and yet was regularly involved in the children's ministry at church. Laurie asked that her husband be removed from ministry until he repented, and if he refused, she asked for the church to support her decision to separate so that Ryan would realize that he could not continue to be destructive in his marriage with no consequences.

Laurie's pastor worked with his leadership to plan a conversation with Ryan, presenting him with these facts as well as reassuring him of their love and commitment for him, Laurie, and their family. They planned to confront Ryan with the evidence of his deceit, his inappropriate relationship with another woman, and his abusive speech to help him come to repentance. If he refused, the next step would be separation, supported by her church. Laurie felt relieved that she was validated, believed, and supported by her church family.

Consult with a Lawyer

You do not need to retain a lawyer at this point, but you do need to talk with one. When you call, ask how much it is for a thirty- or sixty-minute consultation. Go prepared with all your questions written out so that you don't waste time. Learn what your legal rights are as well as legal liabilities if you make certain choices. For example, Sandy was so upset after she discovered her husband's third affair and financial shenanigans that she packed up her stuff, her kids, and fled to her parents' home in another state. Her husband frantically called the police when he came home and everyone had moved out. Sandy got in some legal trouble for moving the kids out of state without her husband's knowledge or permission. In addition to all their marital problems, Sandy now had to hire her own lawyer to get her out of the mess she caused by not getting good legal advice ahead of time.

In the past you may have been afraid to set boundaries or enforce consequences because your husband threatened to cut off financial support or take the children away from you. Knowledge is power. When you know what your legal rights are, you'll be able to make wiser choices because you'll be able to distinguish his lies and threats from what's true. You'll know what you are legally entitled to and protected against so that you aren't as easily intimidated and frightened.

Get Your Own Bank Account and Credit Card

Every woman should apply for a credit card in her own name so that she can establish her own financial history and build a good credit rating. This is especially crucial where there is an imbalance of power and control in the marriage or when the stability of the marriage is shaky. When you take this step, you declare that you will not allow your husband to have control over every aspect of you or your family finances. If you are employed or have money (through an inheritance or other previous assets), you may want to open a separate bank account that assures that you have access to money when you need it.

Prepare to Talk About What Destructive Behaviors You Want Stopped and What Consequences You Will Enforce if He Refuses

Every woman has things in her marriage that she'd like to see stopped or things she'd love to see her husband change. But what are the specific things your husband does or says that you will no longer tolerate? What is so damaging to your marriage, to your children, to you as a person, and to him that you are putting your foot down and saying you can't or won't take it anymore?

Next, figure out what the reasonable consequences should be if he continues that unwanted behavior. I'm not asking you to do anything yet, but you need to determine what your boundaries and the consequences for violating them are. Be careful as you think this through. For example, don't ask your husband to stop doing anything that you are not willing to stop doing also. And don't choose a consequence that you are unable or unwilling to follow through with. Otherwise, you will lose your credibility, and your words won't mean anything.

I can't determine what your deal breakers are or exactly what consequences you will need to implement if he refuses to change. Some relationships are more dangerous and destructive than others. Not every woman living in a destructive marriage fears for her safety or suffers in the same way. You also may not have the same range of options available to you as other women do if your husband refuses to repent. We will talk more about choices and consequences in part 3.

Here are a few examples from women who decided what they would no longer tolerate and the consequences they could implement. Judy said, "I will no longer subject myself to driving with a maniac. His rages in the car terrify me and I'm done. From now on, I am going to drive separately whenever we need to go anywhere until he gets help to control himself."

Janice told me, "I can't live with someone I can't trust. If he isn't going to be honest with me about what's going on, I don't know how to be married to him." Her husband chronically struggled with sexual addiction, Internet pornography, and other things. She hated that every time she caught him in a lie, he'd deny it until she had concrete proof that he couldn't refute. She was willing to be patient with his sexual addiction as she struggled with some of her own besetting sins, but what she wasn't willing to tolerate any longer was his deceit and his refusal to get help. If he still refused, she decided she would need to live separate from him.

Keri said, "I'm unwilling to continue to live with someone I'm afraid of. I am unwilling to be threatened and terrorized. I'm unwilling to live with someone who continually tells me I'm stupid, no good, a piece of work, trash, crazy, and a poor excuse for a mother. If he does it again, I'm calling the police and filing a protection from abuse order."

Abby said, "I will no longer allow him to control everything I do and who my friends are. I work part time, and I can handle it. I want to have friends. I don't like it when he screams at me to get off the phone when I'm chatting with a girlfriend. It's humiliating and I end up avoiding friends. I want to think my own thoughts and have my own opinions and feelings without him telling me I'm wrong or disrespectful and unsubmissive because I see things differently. From now on, I'm not going to keep giving in to him. I'm going to continue to work. I will separate my money from his so he can't control me as much. I will no longer submit to his every whim, and I will emotionally distance myself from him until he chooses to get help."

Lynette said, "I am unwilling to be ignorant of our finances any longer. I need to know how much income he makes, where it is, and how it's spent. I want access to all our accounts. I want to be consulted in moneymaking decisions. I need to be a full partner in this marriage. If he refuses to let me know what's going on, I'm going to separate my income from his and open my own account. I will not allow him to control my money if he's unwilling to be a partner."

Amber said, "I am unwilling to be Mommy to a man who doesn't want to be married, yet wants all the benefits. He doesn't do anything to contribute to taking care of our house, doesn't help with the children, won't hold a steady job, and sits around playing video games all weekend like a ten-year-old boy. I'm done being his wife and mother. It's creepy. If he's not willing to get help and grow up and be responsible, I am going to separate from him."

Prayer Is Your Best Preparation

In all your preparations above, bathe them in prayer. God is on your side, but you do have an enemy who will tempt you to do these very same actions out of spite and revenge. That is not God's way. He wants your husband to come to his senses and to help you both restore your marriage.

> ## Dear God,
>
> *These are tough challenges. I don't know if I can do them without help—real help from real people. Please lead me to the right kind of support. Please help my church leaders be responsive to my needs and give them wisdom to help me in this process. Please help me be strong and protect me and my children from any further hurt.*

Action Step: Make sure you have your safety plan in place and have done the rest of these preparation steps before attempting the tough conversation outlined in chapter 10. This is absolutely crucial.

PART 3

Initiating Changes in Your Marriage

All who do evil hate the light and refuse to go near it for fear their sins will be exposed.

John 3:20, NLT

Nine

Learn to Speak Up in Love

Let not mercy and truth forsake you.

—Proverbs 3:3, NKJV

Jim, a successful corporate executive in his work life, had been attending a ten-week group for men who have been abusive in their intimate relationships. He was also seeing me for individual counseling. At first he refused any kind of help. He didn't think he was that bad. He never beat his wife, and he was never arrested. He said Samantha was abusive too, plus he was a Christian and didn't need psychology; he just needed his wife to stop criticizing him. Jim only acquiesced after Samantha calmly told him he had two choices: he could start personal counseling and attend the group, or he could live alone. The choice was his, but she would not continue to live with him the way he was.

After finishing the ten mandated sessions, Jim told me he volunteered to sign up for the next step, a more intensive twenty-week group. "Wow, Jim," I said. "You seemed so resistant to going there. What happened that helped you want more?"

Jim sat quiet for a moment, his eyes glancing upward to the ceiling. "There were a couple of things," he said. "Hearing the other men's stories gave me the courage to face my problem. I realized my wife was right. I am abusive. But I think one of the most powerful things for me was when the leaders forced me to think about how my wife and daughter felt when I went into one of my rages."

Jim's voice started to crack. He swallowed hard and took a deep breath. "I began to see how scared they must have felt when they watched me smash my fist into the door, scream obscenities, or drive like a crazy man when they were in the car." By now Jim's jaw was taut, his lip quivering, and he was straining to hold back his tears. "I never stopped to think about how my actions affected them before. I only thought about myself."

Jim wiped his brow. "Each week there is a strange combination of tough talk and hard truths, yet it's always delivered in a compassionate way. The two leaders don't let us get away with our excuses, but I don't feel shamed or scolded. I've never experienced anything quite like it. Every week is scary and hard, but good. I think I'm growing. I know one thing: I want to be a better man."

What does it take to get a man like Jim to get it? A man who refused to go for help until given a tough choice? A man who thought his primary problem was that his wife told him things he didn't want to hear? A man who was blind to his own abusive behavior but readily rebuked his wife's sin? What does it take to get a man like Jim not only to want to stop abusing but also to want to be a better man?

I have seen some husbands start to wake up when their wives stop enabling their destructive behaviors through tough consequences and calm, compassionate conversations. Like Samantha, Jim's wife, who told him calmly and empathically he had two choices—he could choose to get help for his abusive behaviors or live alone.

So often, we do it backward. We talk tough, criticize, scream, scold, threaten, and shame our husbands' behaviors or attitudes, but then get compassionate or weak when it comes to implementing the tough consequences of their destructiveness when they refuse to change. When a woman stops being a resentful martyr or a helpless victim and starts living from her CORE, she can learn to become God's warrior to bring about her husband's good. Only from that place is she secure enough in God's love that she's free to love her husband in a courageous way, rather than trying harder to be a good wife.

Men who are habitually destructive refuse to reflect upon their actions or reactions; nor do they take responsibility for them. Their default mode is to blame, accuse, and attack. Everyone else is at fault for what they feel, do, or think. If your man is ever going to change his ways, the first step is he must begin to look within.

Three Nonthreatening Questions to Ask Your Husband

The three questions below are helpful for several reasons. First, they will give you an opportunity to have a different kind of dialogue with your husband, one that may catch him by surprise and allow you to see beyond his anger and defensiveness into a deeper part of his heart. It will help you practice your CORE without the scary part of confrontation. Second, it will give him an opportunity to be self-reflective and more aware of his own thoughts and feelings. Third, his answers (or lack of answers) will give you feedback that will help you to know how to best shape future conversations with him.

When you ask your husband these three questions, I want you to focus your attention on accomplishing two things: listening respectfully and showing undeserved compassion or grace. But remember, that does not mean that you should take responsibility for his problems or enable his destructive behavior to go unchallenged. Your job is to approach your husband humbly (remember your CORE) and listen with as much empathy and respect as you can possibly muster. No jabs, no rolling your eyes, no arguing, no debating his answers as wrong or unfair or saying that you feel that way too.

Our hope in this first step is that he will sense something different in you, a new strength. He sees you are neither resentful nor intimidated. He sees you genuinely care about what he thinks and how he feels as a person, regardless of the type of husband he has been. Pick a time and a place where he will have a moment to stop and think about his answers, and don't demand a response if he doesn't answer right away. Just ask. If he hesitates, you can say lightly, "These are not trick questions. I'm not trying to trap you. I just know we're not doing so well together, and I want to understand you better."

Question 1: Are You Happy?

Your goal with the first question is to hear your husband's feelings and listen compassionately. At the end you want him to feel heard and understood, not judged, shamed, criticized, or condemned.

Don't allow yourself to become defensive or argumentative if you don't like his answer. If your husband says he's happy, you can reply with something like "Wow, I'm surprised by your answer. You don't seem happy much of the time."

Then wait and listen to his response. He might not say anything at all. He might make a cutting remark such as "Well, whenever I'm around you, I'm not happy because you're such a nag or because you never want sex, or _____." You can fill in the blank. Just listen and nod empathically and compassionately. Sincerely try to put yourself in your man's shoes, forgetting for a moment that you are also his wife whom he's hurt.

If his abusive and destructive behaviors were not present in the early years of your marriage but have grown over the years, he may have built up a wall of resentment toward you for reasons you may not be fully aware of. Now is the time to let him talk. Calmly listen. Stand firm in your CORE if he sneers, "No, I'm not happy. Do you think it would take a rocket scientist to figure that out?" Instead of responding with a defensive remark, just listen and show compassion. You could say, "I thought so; you seem unhappy so much of the time." Or "I'm sorry you feel so unhappy." Or "Thanks for telling me. I didn't realize how unhappy you were." Again, don't assume responsibility for his unhappiness; you can't fix it. Simply express compassion for it. The more you listen empathically and don't feel pressured to offer any personal commentary, the better. If he turns it on you and asks you a question, you can say, "I'm not prepared to answer that. Let me give it some thought." If he starts to vent, don't feed his anger, just let it run its course (see Proverbs 15:1). If he starts to verbally attack you, stop the conversation and say, "I'm so sorry. I can't listen very well when you yell at me. I don't want to get defensive or retaliate. I hope we can have this conversation at a later time. I'd really like to hear what you have to say."

Question 2: What Do You See As Our Most Important Goal or Challenge as a Couple If We're Going to Improve Our Relationship?

It's no secret. Even if you've never talked about it, you both know your marriage isn't doing well, especially if he admits that he's not happy. If he names the marriage or you as his reason for his unhappiness, stay calm and listen. After he's finished, you can say something like, "I understand." If he answers the question by saying everything would be fine if you would just be _____ or do _____, press pause. Don't react, but stop and ask yourself whether or not that might be helpful feedback for you. Remember, you are committed to honesty and open to growth and are taking responsibility for yourself (CORE). Ask God whether or not what your husband has told you is true and if it's something you need to or can change.

One of the most common answers I hear from men who are asked this question is that they wish their wives would stop complaining about how often or how much they fall short. When a woman unreservedly tells her man everything about him she is unhappy with, he soon starts to feel as though he can never please her or do anything right. Over time, his motivation to try to please her dissipates and is replaced by a cold wall of indifference and resentment. Put yourself in his shoes for a minute. How would you feel if he constantly criticized and complained about how much you failed to meet his needs? Pretty discouraged, huh? (If you are thinking, *That's exactly what he does,* you already do know how awful it feels!)

On the other hand, you may have already changed dozens of things that he's told you in the past and are quite sure that changing another thing won't make him any happier. If that's the case, you can respond honestly but compassionately, "I don't think my changing more things is really going to make a big difference in our relationship. As soon as I improve in one area, there will always be ten other areas that you think I'm falling short in or that you don't like. I don't think I can ever be the woman you want." In other words, you are letting him know you will never be his fantasy wife and you are committed to honesty, not pretending (CORE).

One of my coaching clients asked her husband this question, and a few days later, he presented her with a list of things he thought they should work on. Here were a few of them:

- Commit to respond positively to each other's feelings.
- Never allow hurt feelings to overcome our faith in each other's commitment in both having and moving toward our goals.
- Never question each other's commitment; only behavior.

- Permit each other to hold the other accountable for moving toward our goals by lovingly presenting comments on current behavior (without relating any behavior in question to anything in the past).

Later she told me during a coaching call that she was not happy with his list. She said, "It all looks good on paper, but he won't do any of them." She felt angry that once again he was going to look like the good guy with all the right answers, and she was left with the same old pattern where nothing actually changed.

I encouraged her to hang in there and, for now, minimize her immediate frustration. Even if he can't do them or doesn't do them, at least she sees what he thinks needs to be done to improve their marriage—things that were actually good answers. She agreed but said, "Then what? What do I do when he doesn't do them?"

I said, "Now you have something objective, something that he has actually put in writing from which to give him truthful feedback on his behavior. For example, when you question him on why he's behaving a certain way and he goes into lockdown mode and gets belligerent toward you, you can say, 'I thought you said that it was important if we are going to improve our marriage to have the freedom to question each other's behavior without questioning our commitment? I'm confused.' This gives him the opportunity to stop and reflect on his actions that don't match his own words, and this is a good place for him to begin to get it. No guarantees, but it's a start."

The third question is the most important.

Question 3: What Kind of Husband and Father Do You Most Desire to Be?

When I asked Jim, the man from the beginning of this chapter, that question, he told me he wished he could be more loving and faithful. When asked that question in the right spirit, I have never, in all my years of counseling, met a man who said his goal was to be the meanest, nastiest husband and father he could be. I've never met a man who said he enjoyed or was proud of behaving like a selfish jerk, a raging maniac, a liar, a cheat, or an insensitive clod. When a man hurts his family, he also hurts himself. God has hard-wired men to want to protect those they love. When they fail, they feel appropriate guilt and shame. Unfortunately, when a man feels these emotions, instead of looking inward to understand why, he often looks for someone to blame and attack. Most of the time that someone is you, because in his mind you (rather than his own behavior) "made him feel bad."

Danielle asked her husband this question, and he responded, "I want to be a good provider." His answer stumped her because he already was a good provider, but he was also demanding, demeaning, and harsh with her and the children. She wasn't sure how to respond, so she said compassionately, "You are definitely a wonderful provider. Is there anything else you wish you were?" He thought for a moment and said, "I wish I were more patient." His answer surprised her. She didn't know her husband wanted to be patient. He always blamed everyone else for his short fuse and clipped-voice tone. Now she knew something that he aspired to.

Your husband's answers to these questions may surprise you. One of my coaching clients said that she was shocked how much her husband opened up to her when she sat quietly on the steps and just listened compassionately to his answers without challenging or arguing or reacting. When he was done, she said she felt closer to him. I'm sure he felt closer to her too. Honest talk, when bathed in compassionate listening, builds intimacy. That is soothing balm for a broken marriage.

Your husband's answers to these questions will shape your future conversations with him, not only in what you say, but more important how you say it.

How We Speak the Truth Is Crucial

What your husband desperately needs is for you to stop pretending every-thing is fine and to tell him the truth. He doesn't need you to collude with his delusion that he's entitled to the perks of a warm and affectionate wife while he behaves as if you're his enemy. He doesn't need you to collude with his delusion that everything he does is great or that there are no consequences for his sinful or destructive behaviors.[1] For his mental, emotional, and spiritual well-being, he needs to live in reality and truth, and that is the only place that he will find healing. But the way you tell the truth can make all the difference in the world as to whether or not he hears you and is willing to take your words to heart. However, keep in mind, even the best truth tellers (like Jesus) are hated and abused by those who prefer darkness to light.

Even the best truth tellers (like Jesus) are hated
and abused by those who prefer darkness to light.

From Jim's experience, as well as most other men and women I've worked with, truth is best received when it's given with compassion, which is why CORE strength is crucial. Unvarnished truth sounds cold, uncaring, and can be hurtful. The Bible tells us that truth spoken with-out love sounds like clanging gongs or clashing cymbals (see 1 Corinthi-ans 13:1). It's ugly noise. It's something you want to run from fast, with your hands clasped tightly over your ears.

Imagine with me that you go to your doctor for a checkup. After the nurse weighs you in and checks your blood pressure, the doctor comes and examines you. After she's done she says, "You're getting fat. You've gained twenty-five pounds. Don't you know that extra weight is dangerous? Your blood pressure is elevated, and you're at a higher risk for coronary artery disease and stroke. Not to mention all kinds of other problems. What's wrong with you?"

How would you feel? Would her truthful words stir your heart to want to lose the weight, or would they incite you to want to get a new doctor or run to the nearest ice cream parlor? It's true that you did gain twenty-five pounds this year and your blood pressure is elevated. But the way your doctor shamed you with the truth didn't motivate you to stop eating or head to the gym, did it?

Now let's imagine that your doctor gave you the same truth, only this time delivered with compassion. She said, "I'm concerned about you and your health. I've seen some troubling changes from last year. What's going on in your life?" Or if she said, "I'm concerned with your weight gain this year. That's not like you. You've always tried hard to manage your weight. What's your biggest challenge in keeping your weight down?" Does that feel different? Would the way she told you the truth help you to face your problem and motivate you to get the weight off, even if it's tough?

The truth often does hurt our feelings, but when we believe that a person is for us and not against us, when they have our best interests at heart, when they want to help us change, it's much easier to listen and think about what he or she said. The psalmist said, "Faithful are the wounds of a friend" (Proverbs 27:6). Tough truth is painful, even when it's delivered with compassion. But when compassion is absent, we feel humiliated, defensive, and angry toward the truth teller, and those negative emotions suck the air right out of our motivation. Instead of spending our energy to solve our problem, we're stuck brooding that someone would dare talk to us that way. In our sin we often retaliate with some ugly words of our own.

Being able to receive truth is tough, but so is being able to speak it wisely. One reason we lose our way in this whole truth-telling arena is we have failed to love our husbands as people created in God's image. We only see them as D-minus husbands. All we see are their failures, mistakes, and sins. We feel angry and hurt that they're not the husbands we want or think we need. We don't know how to love and speak to the men they were created to be, especially when they feel like our enemies.

Let's look at how a woman's truthful words, delivered with humble compassion, influenced a man who was filled with fury and bent on destruction to stop, listen, reflect, and to change his behaviors.

ABIGAIL: A COURAGEOUS WOMAN

The Bible tells us a story of a woman named Abigail who was married to Nabal, a destructive man. He was wealthy but harsh, indifferent, and extremely selfish. Because Nabal was hotheaded and hardhearted, everyone found him difficult to deal with. After David and his men protected Nabal's shepherds in the desert, they asked Nabal for hospitality and nourishment. He refused and instead insulted David.

David, outraged at Nabal's disrespect and the injustice of the situation, vowed to destroy every male in Nabal's household. Hearing David's threats, the servants ran and told Abigail what was happening, seeking her help.

Let's look at Abigail's words and actions to see what she did in a frightening situation. (To read the entire story, see 1 Samuel 25.)

First, Abigail was not passive. When Nabal's servant informed her of her husband's foolish actions, she instantly sprang into action. Abigail did not freeze with fear. Nor did she submit to Nabal's headship and trust God to somehow fix everything. With strength and courage she overruled her husband's decision and instead chose to do the right thing. This was not only for her welfare, but also for Nabal's. She gathered together large quantities of bread and wine, meat and figs, clusters of raisins, and other grains, then loaded them on donkeys and set out to deliver them to David—not knowing if he would kill her too.

When Abigail saw David in the distance, I imagine she felt scared, yet she hastened to meet him. Once there, she bowed low and humbled herself, taking responsibility and apologizing for her husband's surliness. She didn't pretend her husband was any different than he was or make excuses for him. She put her own life on the line to save her household, not knowing what David's response would be toward her boldness. She also did not know what her husband's response would be once he found out she overruled him.

As a result of Abigail's courage, coupled with her humility, David pressed pause on his rage long enough to allow Abigail to speak God's truth into his heart. She reminded David who he was (the Lord's anointed) and encouraged him to respond to Nabal's injustice from the person God called him to be (the future king), rather than how he felt in the moment (rage). Her words helped David reflect on what he was doing and whether or not that was in line with who he was or wanted to be.

As a result of Abigail's intervention, David said, "Blessed is the LORD God of Israel, who sent you this day to meet me! And blessed is your advice and blessed are you, because you have kept me this day from coming to bloodshed and from avenging myself with my own hand" (1 Samuel 25:32–33, NKJV).

Later that same evening, Abigail wisely did not inform her husband of her actions because he was drunk. The next morning she told him what she did, and the Bible says his heart became like stone. Ten days later he was dead.

We will never know if or how Abigail's actions influenced her husband, but we do know that her bravery, humility, and wise words greatly influenced David. Had she shrunk back in fear and done nothing, Nabal and every other male in their household would have been slain. David would have been guilty of murder, forever tarnishing his reputation as the Lord's anointed. Abigail took an enormous risk. Her humble and gentle spirit in approaching David opened his ears and heart to this brave young wife who risked her own life to save her husband and her household. She did Nabal good by doing the right thing, even though in the end, God chose to end his life.

The psalmist said, "Beautiful words stir my heart" (Psalm 45:1, NLT). When you must speak hard truth to your husband, you want it to make an impact, don't you? You want your husband to be able to listen long enough to what you're saying that he would press pause on his destructive behaviors and remember who he is (God's image bearer) and what kind of husband he wants to be (from the third question you asked him). Ultimately, you want to see a change of heart. Harsh, shaming words don't have that power, but beautiful words of truth do.

> *Dear God,*
>
> *I see how beautiful words can stir a heart to want to change. I think I've more often than not spoken harsh, shaming words to my husband when he hurts me. God, give me the right words with the right heart to speak them when the time is right.*

Action Step: Plan how you can use the answers to your three questions to stir your husband's heart with beautiful, yet truthful, words. Hard words need not be harsh. As Abigail did with David, prepare a simple sentence or phrase that would remind him of the person he wants to be rather than criticize his destructive behavior.

For example, Danielle's husband told her he would like to be more patient as a husband and father (from question 3). She thought about it and prepared a sentence or two that she could say when he was expressing irritation or impatience that would help him remember who he wanted to be. A day later, when one of the children spilled his milk during dinner, John started to get harsh. Danielle gently reached over to him and said, "I'll handle this. I know you want to be a more patient dad. Take a few minutes to calm yourself down."

The surprising thing to Danielle is that he did. In that instance her words influenced her husband to reflect on the person he wanted to be rather than react out of how he felt in the moment.

Ten

Stand Up Against the Destruction

Bold love is the active, unnerving pursuit of
the offender to wisely and winsomely incite
reconciliation by exposing the need for
confession, repentance, and restoration.

—Dan Allender

I can't talk with him about any of these things. He won't listen. Or he turns it all back on me," Stephanie said. "I'm exhausted."

If you've been married any length of time, you've probably tried time and time again to have a constructive conversation with your spouse about what he's doing that is hurting you and how you're feeling. You've begged him to get help. For you both to get help. Maybe he's tried for a little bit. But over time, he goes back to his old ways. Nothing's changed.

If you have never had this conversation, if you've never opened your mouth and said, "I don't want you to do that anymore," or "Stop it; that hurts me," then before you stand up against what's happening in your marriage, you must begin with a conversation. Go to my free resource page at www.leslievernick.com/the-emotionally-destructive-marriage and read my article on how to have a difficult discussion with someone.[1] Jesus tells us that when someone offends us, we first go to him privately with what he has done that offends or hurts us (see Matthew 18:15). It's only after we've tried that and there has been no repentance or change that we move to the next level.

You may not feel strong enough to take these next steps just yet. Please don't let that discourage you. When I work with a woman in counseling or coaching, we may take six months or more to develop some CORE strength and document and strategize what the best next steps might be for her, her children, and her marriage. Most things we read, we can't immediately implement. It takes time, practice, and often a supportive coach or counselor who will help you with your next steps. Before takeoff, airline attendants always say in their safety briefing, "If the cabin loses pressure, put your own oxygen mask on first." This good advice applies to your situation too. You can't effectively confront another person if you're not healthy or strong enough to do so. Give yourself time and permission to do what you need to do to get emotionally, spiritually, mentally, and physically prepared to take action.

If your husband has physically abused you or has threatened to hurt you or your children, it is not safe for you to confront him without another person present. It may be dangerous for you to confront him at all. Please consult with an expert in safety planning from one of the resources I've given you in appendix A or your local domestic-violence shelter before taking any action. Continue to document and do the preparation from chapter 8, but you may find that your next step is filing a protection from abuse order and separating, not confronting. Be extremely careful. When a woman separates or threatens to leave an abusive relationship, this can put her in more danger for abuse. That doesn't mean you stay and allow abuse to continue, but it means that if or when you leave, you must do it wisely and with significant planning and preparation.

The Strategy

I'd like to give you a specific way to confront your husband. It is not a magic strategy that is guaranteed to wake him up, but it will help you know what to do, how to handle certain situations, and keep you in control of the conversation. Please feel free to adapt it to your particular situation. As Abigail did with David (from chapter 9), the goal is to surprise your husband with your strength and humility, and God's truth and grace. You want to get your husband's attention and hopefully stir his heart. You want him to see that you are for him, not against him. You want him to know that you want your marriage to survive, but it won't survive if it continues this way. His attitudes and behaviors are unbecoming to him and harmful to you and your relationship with him. You also want to be very clear that if he chooses not to change or get the help he needs to change, there are consequences. You cannot hold your marriage together all by yourself, even if you choose to stay living together in the same house.

> You cannot hold your marriage together all by yourself,
> even if you choose to stay living in the same house.

As with any confrontation, make sure you pick the right time and the right place.[2] Choose a public place, such as a restaurant, where he is less likely to escalate. It's best if you do not drive there with him because if it does not go well, you don't want to have to be trapped in the same car on the way home. If it's in the summer and it's still light outside in the evening, Friday night may be a good time if your husband works a normal workweek. If you have children living at home, make arrangements for them to sleep elsewhere Friday night. You don't want them to be subjected to the aftereffects at home if it does not go well. You also must at least make a tentative plan for you to sleep elsewhere Friday night if your husband is not receptive to what you say and becomes destructive.

Inform your support team of the time, date, and place you are going to talk with your husband. If you have any concern for your safety, you should ask someone from your support team to accompany you and be present during the confrontation, or at least be in the same place off to the side so that you are not alone. Have your cell phone with you and on vibrate. They will be praying for you and calling you thirty minutes from the time you start, to check on your well-being. When they call, answer it. Tell your husband that your support team has been praying for you both during this conversation and they're checking on your well-being. This demonstrates you have support, you have told people what's going on, and you are not turning back. Keep the call brief; they will call you again in thirty minutes.

The confrontation should not take long and might even be over before your support team phones you. Do not allow yourself to get drawn into an argument about what you do wrong, or a debate on the merits of your statements. Some manipulative distractions he might use are:

- You just want your way.
- You're just as much at fault for our marriage mess as I am.
- You're breaking up the family.
- I can't believe you're so cold and heartless.
- You think you're better than me.
- Who have you been talking to? This isn't you.

It's tempting to get sidetracked, get defensive, and answer those distractions. Don't. You will lose your way, and he will gain the upper hand, because now he's in control of the topic. What you are going to say is not open for discussion. The reason for this confrontation is for him to listen to what you have to say and to decide whether or not he's willing to agree and comply. He may need time to think about what you've said, and if so, tell him he has twenty-four hours to get back to you. Do not return home during that time or allow the children to return home. Let him feel what it's like to be all alone without his family.

Open the conversation with this statement: "Thank you for being willing to meet with me. I appreciate it. This won't take long, but I need you to listen to what I have to say. When I'm done, you can respond, but please don't interrupt. Are you willing to do that?" If he refuses, simply say, "I'm sorry. I had hoped you would be interested in what I had to tell you." Then get up and gather your things to leave. If he stops you, simply ask again, "Are you willing to listen to what I have to say?" You want to remain calm and in control. If he tries to gain control, you simply stand up again and say, "I thought you were willing to listen; if not, I'll have to leave." Usually he's curious and surprised enough at your calm control that he'll agree to listen.

Begin your talk with the positives about the man you fell in love with, the things you appreciate about him, the good things about your marriage (if any).

Joanne (chapter 5) told her husband, "When I first fell in love with you, I had a fairy-tale idea about how our marriage would be. You were handsome, strong, and so smart. I felt like I was the luckiest girl alive. You still are incredibly attractive, and I appreciate how hard you work to support our family financially."

He'll enjoy this, so he'll likely not interrupt.

Next, humbly share a few things about yourself, such as what you've been working on to grow or what you've learned about yourself, as well as that you are for him and for your marriage. For example, Joanne continued, "I haven't been a perfect wife, God knows, but I've come to realize that there is no perfect wife or spouse. But I have worked hard over the years to be a better wife. I think I've learned how to communicate more effectively and not lash out in anger when you or the kids disappoint or fail me. I want you to know I still love you, and I want to see us be a happy couple, but now it's up to you."

At this time you are going to pull in some of his answers to the three questions you asked from chapter 9. For example, you can acknowledge he's not happy. If he suggested some things that the two of you could do to improve your relationship, you can say that you appreciate that he wants to make things better. You want to remind him of the man he said he wanted to be and then present him with hard facts and specific ways he is not living up to his own values or aspirations.

He will not listen long because this part will be painful, so do your homework and be prepared. If there are a number of "intolerable" behaviors that you want changed, your husband may not be able to listen to them all at once. It would be too overwhelming, and he'll get defensive because he'll feel like he is being ganged up on. Pick the most important and start there. If he's receptive, you can talk more. If he's not, there is no sense in bringing up the rest. You also want to make sure your tone is neutral, not sharp or shaming, or he won't listen at all.

Joanne was never able to get Darryl to answer the third question about what kind of husband and father he wanted to be, so she dug back to some things he said early on in their marriage about how much he valued honesty, loyalty, and companionship, and so she used those in her confrontation.

Joanne continued. "I remember that when we first got married, you told me that your highest values were honesty, companionship, and loyalty. But you haven't been honest with me. I ran a credit check on you and found out that you are fifteen thousand dollars in debt with a credit card I don't know anything about. You've refused to share your bank account information with me, yet you require me to give you a detailed summary of everything I spend. You feel entitled to call me names or ridicule me when I make a mistake or do something you think is dumb. When we were walking together two weeks ago, and I was going too fast, you yanked me back to my place as if I were a dog on a leash. If I did or said any of those things to you, you'd be outraged and wouldn't stand for it."

Joanne concluded her confrontation with, "I am your partner, your wife, your lifelong companion; yet I feel like you treat me as if I'm your servant or a dog. That doesn't work for me. It hurts me, it hurts our marriage, and it diminishes you. That is not how a man of loyalty or honesty behaves."

Joanne stopped talking and let Darryl absorb what she said. She had never been this direct, this bold, this courageous before. He was taken aback by her strength and confidence and agreed that he was wrong and needed to make some changes. He said he loved her too and wanted their marriage to work. Joanne didn't accept Darryl's words without some specific action steps included.

Most confrontations result in some kickback as to what you need to change too. There is blaming: "If you didn't do this, I wouldn't have done that." Don't let yourself get swept into arguing or defending yourself. Simply say, "I'm sure there are things I need to change, and if you want to share with me specific things I do that bother you, I would be willing to listen. But right now these are the things that I need you to change if we're going to repair our marriage. Are you willing?"

The Commitment

Joanne handed Darryl a printed bulleted summary she had prepared earlier that highlighted the attitudes and behaviors she wanted Darryl to change. She asked him to read it in front of her as confirmation that he understood what she said and was going to agree to what needed to change on his end to repair their relationship. It said:

- I agree I will use respectful language in your presence: no sarcasm, screaming, mocking, ridicule, or cursing at you or the children.
- I agree I will never destroy your possessions or the children's things.
- I agree I will never touch you or the children in anger.
- I agree I will share with you all financial records, bank accounts, credit cards, and passwords, and we will work together to make our budget and have mutual accountability for our spending.
- I commit to change these destructive attitudes and behaviors so that our marriage can be reconciled.
- I will seek an accountability partner within ten days who will help me toward these goals.
- If I don't follow through, or I slip back into these destructive patterns, I will accept feedback from you.
- I will take responsibility to go to counseling and attend a group for abusive men in order to get the additional help I need to change.

Darryl tried to negotiate the terms of the last two statements, but Joanne stayed firm. She said she'd put up with his destructive behavior long enough and if their marriage was going to be repaired, he would need to agree to these changes. Joanne gave him a copy of the commitment paper and kept one for herself. Darryl was in shock.

Two weeks later, Darryl began to slip and ridiculed her in front of the children. Immediately, she pulled out her paper to remind him of their talk. Darryl got defensive and told Joanne she was being too critical, but Joanne remained firm, calm, and controlled. She spoke from her CORE. She told Darryl if their marriage was going to heal, he would need to stop these behaviors. If he wasn't capable of stopping them, he'd need to get outside help. She was no longer going to put up with them. They were too destructive to their marriage.

Time will tell whether Darryl will follow through with the necessary changes needed to be the man he says he wants to be and restore their marriage. But either way, Joanne has a plan and has worked with God and trusted advisors to put her marriage in its proper place, center herself in God, and develop her CORE strength. These things will help her get through whatever happens.

What to Do If It Does Not Go Well

Many confrontations do not go well. Your husband might be proud and rebellious. He might be afraid. He might be lazy, selfish, and foolish. He doesn't understand what you're doing or why you're changing, but it throws him off his game. His first attempt will be to get you to back down and revert to your old ways of placating and accommodating because you're afraid of his reaction. If that doesn't work, he'll try to provoke you to start yelling and screaming so that you look unstable or like the one who is wrong. Stay calm.

In the past, he has not been open to truth or help, so why would anything be different now? That doesn't mean he can never change; it's just going to take a strong, consistent stance on your part with some tough consequences put in place. Here's how to handle the situation if and when it starts to deteriorate.

While you're talking, if he starts interrupting you or becoming destructive in any way (such as rolling his eyes, reading the menu, mocking you), stop talking, stand up, and say in a firm but calm tone, "If you don't stop _____ (describe whatever destructive or abusive behavior he's doing), I'm going to leave this restaurant." If he stops, say, "Are you willing to listen to me?" If he agrees, sit down and start again. If he refuses, leave the public place, get in your car, lock your doors, call your support group and let them know what happened, then drive to the place you arranged to stay. If he follows you, drive directly to the police station instead. (Know where it is ahead of time.) If he tries calling you, do not answer. He is not in control of this situation; you are. Let him sit with the consequences of his decision not to respect you and listen when you asked him. The next day, when you're ready, call him back and ask him if he's willing to hear you this time. If so, try again in a public place, the same way. If not, then you will need to move on to the consequences stage.

CONSEQUENCES

Sadly, some men will not change their ways even when given direct and specific feedback that their attitudes and behaviors are hurtful, sinful, or destructive. The Bible describes these people as fools and as evildoers. A woman whose husband refuses to obey God is instructed to influence him by her own godly behavior (see 1 Peter 3:1–2). That does not mean sacrificing yourself and allowing your husband's abuse to continue. In some cases, it means all you can do is love him enough to get out of the way and allow him to experience the consequences of his sin, and pray that the pain will shock him awake.

The apostle Paul describes an important biblical truth that we often fail to apply in marriage. It's called the law of consequences. He wrote, "Don't be misled—you cannot mock the justice of God. You will always harvest what you plant. Those who live only to satisfy their own sinful nature will harvest decay and death from that sinful nature. But those who live to please the Spirit will harvest everlasting life from the Spirit" (Galatians 6:7–8, NLT). Elsewhere Paul tells believers to distance themselves from other believers who live idle lives, who are lazy, undisciplined, and who refuse to work. He says to do this for the purpose of bringing them to their senses (see 2 Thessalonians 3:6–15).

Somehow people have gotten the idea that marriage voids God's law of consequences, except in the cases of adultery and perhaps physical abuse. Counselors and pastors often advise a wife that God calls her to suffer in her marriage while continuing to provide all the privileges and benefits of marriage regardless of how her husband treats her, provides for her, or violates their marital vows. This stance only reinforces the delusion of the destructive spouse who believes he can do as he pleases with no consequences. Marriage does not give someone a "get out of jail free" card that entitles a husband to lie, mistreat, ignore, be cruel, or crush his wife's God-given dignity. To believe otherwise is not to know the heart of God.

> Marriage does not give someone a "get out of jail free" card that entitles a husband to lie, mistreat, ignore, be cruel, or crush his wife's God-given dignity without any consequences.

It's important that we distinguish consequences from punishment. For example, when a child refuses to listen to his parent and puts his hand on a hot stove, the consequence is the burning pain. It is meant to teach the child not to put his hand on a hot stove again. The parent may still punish the child for not listening. It is not your job to punish your spouse, nor is it appropriate. However, painful consequences for sinful behaviors are designed to teach us not to repeat the same behaviors over and over again. When we tell a woman she must nullify the painful consequences for her destructive husband, we not only hurt her, but we hurt him. He won't learn, grow, or stop his destructive ways.[3]

Here are a few examples of possible consequences when your husband is destructive:

1. *End a conversation.* When he becomes verbally aggressive, walk away. Remind him that you will not allow yourself to be talked to that way. Do not argue with those boundaries. If he follows you, go to a room with a door and lock the door. If he's been violent in the past, don't go to a room without a window or exit. Leave the house. Always make sure you carry a cell phone with you and have it preprogrammed to 911. If you feel frightened by his behavior, call the police.

2. *Refuse to drive anywhere together.* If he has been known to verbally assault you in a car, drive recklessly, or drink too much alcohol, do not get in a car with him. Drive separately, because he can't control himself and won't learn self-control. He loses the privilege of your company in the car when he mistreats you or scares you.

3. *Exit a situation when he is escalating.* Leave the room or leave the house if you feel things are heating up. If you haven't already, you need to get your safety plan in place now, before you need to implement it. That might mean putting a spare car key in the garage or under a planter, packing a suitcase and hiding it in the trunk or garage, making sure your children know that when you say a certain phrase, they all exit the house and get into the car. If you've been through the cycle, you can tell when he's getting worked up. You don't have to stay for the blowup stage. Leave. The consequence for his inability to control his temper and his tongue (or his hands) is the loss of your company (for an hour, for an evening, for a season).

4. *Initiate church discipline.* Most churches are reluctant to do this, but it's worth checking into. If your husband is on staff

at the church or in a prominent leadership role, it's crucial that you have documented evidence of his destructive behaviors, as these become your required witnesses as shown in Matthew 18:15–17. The church leadership can mandate him into counseling or can support other consequences to help him wake up to his destructive behaviors.

5. *Withdraw sexual privileges.* Sexual intimacy in marriage is designed to be an expression and symbol of love and safety. When someone is repeatedly destructive toward you without remorse or repentance, being forced to engage in sex causes you to feel like an object or worse. If he does not choose to value you as his wife, your loving relationship is broken.[4] Without repair, to have sex is to pretend, to go through the motions, and to confuse him that his sin was not that bad.

6. *Separate.* This could be separate sleeping quarters, emotionally distancing yourself, separating your finances, or asking him to move out of the home. When your husband repeatedly refuses to listen to feedback about his destructive behaviors, and you are in a position to do so, separation can be a very effective consequence. It has the potential to "wake him up" and let him know that he cannot continually act abusively toward you and expect that you will still want to be in a loving relationship with him. Separating often begins to open the abuser's eyes for the first time that you are an individual with your own thoughts, your own feelings, and your own needs. Your husband will often not take you seriously or give meaningful consideration to changing his destructive ways until he is quite sure you are willing to live without him.

7. *Call the police.* Call and press charges if he is physically abusive, threatening, or is destroying pets or property. Do the same if he's involved with illegal activities, such as drugs or theft. The longer you make excuses or put up with it, the more deceptive and/or aggressive he will become. Spending time in jail can help him see that what he is doing is not only wrong but illegal, and that you will not allow yourself or your children to be threatened, harassed, or physically abused.

Psychologist Henry Cloud wrote, "Do not hope for the evil persons to change. It could happen, and it does, *but it does not happen by giving in to them, reasoning with them, or giving them another chance to hurt you.* It happens when they finally are subject to limits that force them to change."[5]

WHY DOES HE DO WHAT HE DOES?

You may be wondering why I haven't talked about the reasons men abuse, deceive, disrespect, or act indifferently toward their wives. Is it a result of mental illness? personality disorder? difficult childhood? brain injury? posttraumatic stress? addiction? Asperger syndrome? poor impulse control? hierarchical cultural norms? wrong thinking and beliefs about women? sin?[6]

Take your pick. There could be some aspects of any or all those problems. However, most wives know that their husbands do not act destructively in other settings because they know they would experience serious consequences if they did. Most experts in family abuse say these abusive and destructive behaviors are not irrational but purposeful. They are aimed at controlling their intimate partner.[7] That doesn't mean that there aren't other issues going on that need to be addressed, but those issues are secondary to the idea of male privilege, where a man believes he is the king in his kingdom (home) and therefore is entitled to rule and punish to get his way.

Whatever the reason behind your husband's actions, in the end does it matter? If you are threatened, physically abused, repeatedly lied to, cheated on, verbally battered, humiliated, ignored, or intimidated, it matters little *why* he acts the way he does. If you want any hope for the marriage to survive, he has to recognize that he has a problem, want to change, and be willing to receive the help he needs in order to stop his destructive behaviors. Meanwhile, your main responsibility in these instances is to make sure you and your children are healthy and safe, and not to enable your husband to continue to sin, or cover up for him, or frantically duct tape your marriage together.[8]

Dear God,

This is so scary, but it's also freeing. For the first time I see your plan for healing broken relationships. I need to do the right thing, and it's not to close my eyes and stay silent. It's to confront him. But I need your help. I'm afraid it won't go well and I will have to implement a consequence. Help me be strong.

Action Step: Jeremiah says, "Your own conduct and actions have brought this upon you. This is your punishment. How bitter it is! How it pierces to the heart!" (Jeremiah 4:18, NIV). What specific consequences do you need to put in place if your spouse refuses to change?

Eleven

When There Is No Obvious Change

For my enemies refuse to change their ways;
they do not fear God.

—Psalm 55:19, NLT

I am done. In the last two days, my husband said I'm worthless, I'm lazy, and he hates me—all in front of our three kids. I don't know how much more of this I can take." Francine sighed. "My boys cursed me out today. I'm afraid they're learning to be just like him."

"You've been living like this for a long time," I said.

"I know. I just don't know what God wants me to do. I've read book after book that tells me to stay the course and try to love him no matter what. Several pastors have told me the same thing. They say, 'Stay and choose to be happy despite your circumstances.'"

"Do you think you can do that?" I asked.

"I've tried. I don't sit around crying all day. I'm generally a happy person, except when he's around. Don't get me wrong. He's not a total loser. He's a hard worker, loves his kids, even though he says things to them that no parent should say to a child. He tells them they're fat, stupid, and will never amount to anything. But he lies to me about all kinds of things. When I catch him, he says he lies so I won't nag or throw a fit. He treats me like I'm his servant. No respect at all. His father is the same kind of person. I see where he learned how to treat women, but that doesn't make it right! I have asked him to go to counseling on a number of occasions, but he refuses and says he never will. I feel like I'm in a sinking boat. If I don't grab the kids and jump off, we're all going to go under."

Francine's words remind me of many women who have tried to invite change into their marriages, but nothing changes. He refuses to get help. He continues to lie, to spew his rage all over you, to tell you what you can and can't do, and to manipulate and blame you. He's foolish and irresponsible, may frighten you and the children, and demands accountability but gives none in return. On top of all this, he regularly pulls out the "God hates divorce" card to remind you that you can't divorce him. Now what? You're legally married, but you have no relational marriage. I liken it to wandering around the dark shadows of Nowhere Land.

However, I want you to know you *do* have choices to make—important choices that will affect you and others for years to come.

CHOOSE WISELY

Many women continue to feel helpless, angry, and victimized because they believe or have been told that they have no choices. They believe that God says that they must stay living with their destructive spouse, no matter what. That's not true. You have choices not only on what actions to take, but also on what attitudes you will embrace.

Not all conservative biblical scholars or pastors agree on what constitutes biblical grounds for separation or divorce. Indeed, it can become very confusing to read through their points of view to discern whose perspective is right or more true to the Scriptures. Here is where you will have to do some thinking and digging and praying on your own.

There may be people around you who tell you what God says you must do. Their motives are usually good. They want to help. They care. They're afraid for you and your family. And they want to remain true to God's Word. Therefore they all have their opinion on what God says is best for you.[1]

You have choices not only on what actions to take,
but also on what attitudes you will embrace.

It may be tempting for you to abdicate your decision-making responsibility to your pastor or counselor, or someone who wrote a book on marriage and divorce. If your husband has controlled you and made all your significant choices, you are not used to making decisions on your own. However, to become healthier, you must now learn how to make wise choices. That does not mean you don't seek godly counsel or read helpful books, but you also must do the work to understand what God's Word says to you about your situation. You must come to terms with the reality that whether you stay or whether you leave, there will be people who believe you made the wrong choice and will have no reservations telling you so.

It's crucial that as you make your decision about what to do, you need to think through the potential risks and consequences of your choice. What will it cost you and your children to stay living in the same toxic environment, and what will it cost you to leave? This decision is so important because it will affect you and your family for the rest of your lives.

As you've read through this book, you've heard the words of women who have been on the verge of emotional, physical, mental, financial, and spiritual collapse while living with destructive spouses. It is important that you know that "wife abuse accounts for 25 percent of suicides by all U.S. women, and 50 percent of suicides by African-American women"[2]

The National Institute of Mental Health reports, "Lack of an intimate, confiding relationship, as well as overt marital disputes, have been shown to be related to depression in women. In fact, rates of depression were shown to be highest among unhappily married women."[3] Psychologist David Goleman says science has now demonstrated that relationships don't just mold our experience; they mold our biology too. He wrote, "Nourishing relationships have a beneficial impact on our health, while toxic ones can act like slow poison in our bodies."[4]

> You must come to terms with the reality that whether you stay or whether you leave, there will be people who believe you made the wrong choice and will have no reservations telling you so.

Jeanine told me, "I thought staying for my kids was a good idea, but now I see the damage it caused them. As adults, they are all either victims or abusers. The pattern has repeated. I wish I would have made a different choice."

The Center on Child Abuse and Neglect at the University of Oklahoma reports that "children who witness violence in their home are six times more likely to commit suicide, twenty-four times more likely to commit sexual assault, 50 percent more likely to abuse drugs and alcohol, and 74 percent more likely to commit crimes against others."[5] If your children are being abused, or if they witness you being abused, the price to stay is too costly. Studies show children fare better when their parents stay together, unless there is abuse.[6]

Yet leaving a destructive marriage is not pain free. It, too, has costs and consequences. Financially you may not be as well off. Your children will have to be in your spouse's care without your supervision during visitation. Depending on his propensity for retaliation and his financial resources, he can make your life miserable by repeatedly taking you to court regarding issues with the children. In addition, new challenges, such as living alone for the first time, finding a new church family, or starting a career in midlife, can be quite frightening for some women and may feel more stressful than figuring out how to stay with a destructive spouse.

Every woman in a destructive marriage must wrestle with what she believes God says to her about her situation. Circumstances vary, even in a destructive marriage. The Bible doesn't always tell us exactly what to do. The best way we can discern as finite, limited, sinful people is to read God's Word for ourselves, pray for God's wisdom, consult with people we respect, and walk humbly with God in this journey. The Bible tells us that "we walk by faith, not by sight" (2 Corinthians 5:7). We can't always see where we are going, but we still walk, trusting that God is leading us and guiding us forward. Trusting God through this process is like traveling with my GPS. I have faith that it is going to take me where I need to go, even if I don't exactly know how. I listen to the instructions and do the next thing. If I make a wrong turn, it doesn't stop working or say, "Stupid, what did you do that for?" It gently says, "Recalculating." As I continue to listen to its directions, I will find my way, even if I make ten wrong turns in the process.

In the same way, God gives us a GPS (I call it God's Positioning System) and instructs us how to walk by faith. God's GPS is the Bible, the Holy Spirit, and wise and godly people. When we make a wrong turn, we can trust that God will tell us to recalculate. We can trust him to show us the right path. He says, "I will instruct you and teach you in the way you should go; I will counsel you with my eye upon you" (Psalm 32:8). When we make a wrong turn, we can trust that he will help us recalculate and get back on the right path.

One more thing you need to be aware of: whatever choices you make, whether you stay, whether you separate, or whether you divorce, be prepared for more suffering and grief ahead. Your decisions will bring challenges and criticism from those who think you're making the wrong choice. Your choices will bring opportunities for growth as well as temptations to sin. Knowing that these stumbling blocks and stepping stones are ahead of you will help you keep your eyes open so that you can be more vigilant over your heart and mind as you wrestle through some tough decisions.

IF YOU CHOOSE TO STAY, CHOOSE TO STAY WELL

There are many reasons a woman decides to stay, some healthy and some not. She stays because she's embarrassed and doesn't want anyone to know what's going on at home. She stays because she doesn't want her children to experience a broken home. She stays because she has more financial security staying than starting over. She stays because she believes or has been told that she has no biblical grounds to leave. She stays because she thinks she'll be a poor example of a Christian if she says she can't take it anymore. She stays because she's too afraid to do anything else. She stays because she thinks it is what she's supposed to do. She stays because she fears God will be disappointed or angry with her if she leaves and fears he'll punish her with someone or something worse.

I hope by now you've worked through some of the things in these chapters so that if you stay, you will stay for good reasons and in God's strength. Over the thirty years I've been doing counseling, I've met many individuals, both men and women, who have stayed in destructive marriages, but they remained bitter, angry, spiteful, depressed, and resentful. They demonstrated no peace, joy, or hope in their countenance or with their decision. They were filled with fear and contempt, not with Christ's love or peace. Staying that way is a terrible choice, and it does not bring any pleasure to God.

Abigail (chapter 9) was a woman who stayed, and stayed well. The Bible describes her as a beautiful and intelligent person. Abigail thrived despite her husband's surliness. Their servants respected her, and when they saw Nabal made a foolish decision, they immediately turned to Abigail. They had confidence she would know what to do (see 1 Samuel 25).

Abigail neither pretended nor made excuses for her husband's foolishness. She lived in truth without bitterness. She had the courage and humility to take appropriate action to right Nabal's wrong decisions without rancor. She practiced living from her CORE. But let's look at a few other things Abigail must have done in order to stay well.

1. Abigail Let Go of Her Dream of Having a Loving Husband or Marriage Even Though She Was Still Married

Abigail nurtured no fantasies of Nabal becoming a loving partner. She accepted who he was, grieved her loss, and moved on. She had no expectations of him other than to be what he was. Abigail practiced something that many women who choose to stay fail to do. She stopped emotionally investing in trying to get her husband to change. Perhaps he was unwilling. Maybe she realized he was incapable. Instead, she used her energies to keep strong and sane and built her best life within the circumstances she was in.

Perhaps you've acknowledged that you're in a destructive marriage, but you still have not accepted it. You're stuck in your anger, thinking that this is not how things should be. You're right, but when you refuse to accept what is, you aren't able to move through your anger and start grieving your losses.

Grieving is something we don't know how to do very well, and we avoid it because it's so painful. Many women in destructive marriages are unable to let go of their fantasy that somehow their husbands will become the men they long for and that their relationships will change. Although their marriage relationships have died, they lurk around the gravesite, hoping for a resurrection. They tell themselves, *After all, God can work miracles, and he is the God of the resurrection.* And that's true. God could resurrect your relationship. But if and when that happens, you'll know it and it will look very different to you. Meanwhile, grieve, let go, and move on, even though you choose to stay legally married.

Grief is painful, but the good news is that there is always new life after death. Spring always follows winter. Even after a horrific fire has ravaged the forest and everything looks black and bleak, before too long, tiny bluebells poke their heads out of the loamy soil and feathery green shoots of fern appear where none had been before. Now that sunlight is able to reach the forest floor, new growth blossoms. That new growth was not possible when the thick foliage of the trees shaded the forest bottom. In a similar way, your marriage relationship has burned down to the ground, but that doesn't mean that your life is over and that there isn't something new that God wants to blossom in you out of the ashes of your broken marriage.

2. Abigail Remained God-Centered, Not Husband-Centered or Self-Centered

We can see by Abigail's humility and resourcefulness that she depended on a strength outside of herself for wisdom and courage. She knew what to do in order to live by faith, not by fear or anger. She leaned hard into God's grace. Although she was not loved by her husband, Abigail knew she was loved and valued by God, and she felt secure in that. She trusted God's wisdom to guide her steps. She had a ministry to Nabal, not a relationship with him. If you choose to stay, God still has a role for you to play in your husband's life. It will look more like ministry than marriage, but with God's help, you can find peace and purpose, even though you don't receive love and companionship from your spouse.

3. Abigail Did Not Allow Her Husband's Surliness to Infect Her with Its Poison

This is perhaps the most difficult part of staying well with a destructive person. He spews toxic gas all over the house, and you can't help but breathe it in. If you're not careful, it will poison your heart. You start to become just as hardhearted and foolish as the destructive person has been. Or, in your attempts to protect yourself, you distance yourself with walls of resentment and bitterness. Either way, your spirit shrinks and you cannot thrive. You can barely breathe.

Living from your CORE, daily prayer, and putting on the armor of God (see Ephesians 6:10–20) is like wearing a protective gas mask when toxic gas is present. It will keep you from being poisoned. However, even with a good gas mask in place, sometimes toxic fumes are too potent or are around too long, and you are still overcome.

One of the red flags that indicates you are not staying well is that you are breaking down either physically, emotionally, mentally, or spiritually, and are not able to bounce back. If that is the case, you might need to reconsider your choice to stay.

When I wrote my book *The Emotionally Destructive Relationship*, I shared my personal story about my relationship with my biological mother. She divorced my father when I was eight. When I was fourteen, she lost custody of us to my father because of her alcoholism and abusive behaviors. She chose not to have much contact with us over the years. Even as an adult and a Christian counselor, I found it impossible to have a constructive conversation with her. When she verbally assaulted me, I didn't know how to protect my heart, and I would easily get infected with her poison. I began lobbing my own verbal bombs right back. I also struggled with depression, self-hatred, and self-pity. I needed time away from the relationship and space to heal. I had to work on letting go and grieving my loss of not having the kind of mother, or grandmother for my children, that I wanted. I needed to learn how to forgive her and heal from the hurts she inflicted. During that time, I drew close to God and learned how not to retaliate or pay back evil for evil. These lessons are not mastered in a month, but over years.

I say this to you because you, too, may need space and time away from your destructive spouse. You know you're not doing well. Stress and distress affects us all in various ways. One client found her body couldn't take it anymore. She suffered with irritable bowel syndrome, high blood pressure, and chronic fatigue. Another client, Jane, kept asking me if she would need to stay on her antidepressants and self-medications just to stay living with her husband. She said, "I don't want to have to numb myself with Xanax and alcohol just to stay in the same house as my husband. I don't think God wants that for me, and I won't do it anymore." God cares for your safety and your sanity, and if you can't stay well, you may need to separate for a season or even permanently.

If You Choose to Separate, Choose to Separate Well

Cindy was a young, attractive, athletic woman with two small children in tow. When I met her in my waiting room, she glanced up while pushing icons on her iPad and said, "I'm sorry. I couldn't find a baby-sitter, but I needed this appointment. They'll watch videos here in your waiting room, if that's okay with you."

"Sure," I said, greeting the children.

Cindy walked into my office, sat down, and opened up her folder with pages of scribbled, yellow-lined notepaper. "I have a lot to discuss with you," she said. "I don't know what to do anymore. I've been to two pastors, one marriage mentor, and a Christian counselor, and I hear the same thing over and over."

"What do you hear?" I asked, curious.

"My husband's always had an anger problem. Before we got married, we talked about it in our premarital counseling," she said. "He agrees it's something he needs to work on. He knows he shouldn't lose his temper, but somehow or other it always comes back to a problem with me. He says I provoke him."

"Do you think you provoke him?" I said.

"I'm sure I do at times," Cindy said. "I'm spunky and outspoken. But I don't think I deserve to be slapped or punched or the kids screamed at until they pee in their pants. I'm tired of it, and I want him to move out."

"You want to separate?" I said.

"Yes, but everyone tells me that if I changed and was less direct, less confrontational, he wouldn't act that way. I'm sick and tired of his anger being my problem. I don't want my kids seeing him act that way. They're scared and I'm scared."

"What stops you from asking Nate to move out?"

"I know our church will disapprove. I won't have any support. They'll be on his side," she said. "He's a great guy everywhere but home."

"That makes it harder," I said. "Any other reasons?"

"I don't know how to do it. What are the rules? How long should he stay away?" Cindy said. "I don't want a divorce; I just want him to get help. I want him to stop."

I explained the following information to Cindy.

Basic Reasons for Separation

Many Christian leaders dislike the idea of separation when a marriage is in trouble. They believe this temporary solution makes the marriage worse. True, separating does add new temptations and issues to the marital mess already present. However, separation is a wise choice when you are afraid, in danger, or feel as though you have to check yourself into the hospital because you can't take it anymore. Or, as with Cindy, separation may be the only way your husband hears that if he wants to stay married, he will need to make serious changes. All other attempts to communicate that truth have failed.

Separation is never a good choice when you are tired of being married, you want to go off and find yourself, or you'd like to try the single life for a while to see if you still want to be married. I've provided written guidelines for a biblical separation that you can download at www.leslievernick.com/the-emotionally-destructive-marriage. If you are planning to separate, give a copy to your pastor or counselor so that he or she understands why you're taking these steps and can offer the support and accountability you and your husband need.

One of the risks a woman takes when she separates is that her husband may decide he's done. He is not willing to change. If he is not willing to do any work, he may contact his own attorney, file for divorce, start dating other women, withdraw financial support, or simply let things ride in limbo as long as you are willing. Therefore, before you take such a step, make sure that living with the consequences of divorce is less damaging to you and your children than continuing to live in a destructive marriage.

Basic Rules for Separation

Separation is for the purpose of your safety, bringing your spouse to his senses, and giving you space and time to heal. It may last a few weeks or six months or longer. It gives you and your spouse time to work on your own issues, without the stress of living together. When handled wisely and both parties are willing to do the work, it can be an excellent strategy to bring healing to a destructive marriage.

Separation is not an opportunity to date others or explore new relationships. This is a temptation when you are hurting and lonely, but it is a grave danger to you and your marriage. If you become emotionally hooked into a new love relationship, you will get distracted from your goals. A new relationship always feels easier, more exciting and appealing than repairing your marriage, because there is no baggage or old history to work through. If your husband wakes up as a result of your separation and wants to work on himself so that your marriage can be restored, you will be conflicted and less likely to want to work on your marriage if you've invested your heart in another man.

Separating also requires that you talk with your spouse about financial support, custody, and visitation of the children, if and what you are going to tell friends and family, and what needs to happen or change before he can return to the home. If talking constructively together has never gone well before, have these conversations with a third party present to help you reach agreement and bear witness to what was decided.

Is Divorce Ever a Biblical Option?

When the Pharisees asked Jesus why Moses allowed divorce, Jesus told them that from the beginning that was not God's intent. God designed marriage to be a lifetime relationship. Moses permitted divorce only as a concession to people's hard hearts. God's ideal for marriage hasn't changed. He still wants it to be a lifetime relationship, but hard hearts still cause serious wounds to people and relationships. There are times it is just not wise or safe to stay married if the destructive person has not had a change of heart. They would have too much power to continue to hurt you.

For example, Dana filed for divorce soon after she realized that the affair her husband promised to end two years ago never ended. He was living a double life, and the entire time she thought he was working on "reconciling" their relationship, he was still in contact with the other woman. No amount of talk or time was going to rebuild her shattered trust. If he could lie so convincingly to her, their pastor, and their counselor, how would she ever believe anything he ever said to her?

In another case, after forty years in an unhappy marriage, Betty and her husband were nearing retirement. She wasn't sure how she would be able to handle his indifference toward her once he was no longer working. As she was gathering information to take to a financial planner, Betty discovered that over the past ten years, her husband had withdrawn their savings, withdrawn her inheritance from her parents, and emptied his retirement accounts. When she confronted him, he acted as though the bank made a mistake or that he didn't know what she was talking about. Betty combed through other records and realized that he owed the IRS over fifty thousand dollars for back taxes for liquidating his retirement accounts. Harold continued to play the victim of identity theft, incorrect tax records, and computer glitches. Eventually Betty gathered proof, finding his signature on withdrawals he made.

Betty was furious and scared. Everything they had saved was gone, and now they had this huge debt owed to the IRS. What was she going to do? She couldn't trust her husband. She didn't believe a word he said. She had no idea what he did with all that money. But she knew one thing: she did not want to live another day or sleep another night in the same house with this stranger.

Divorce was the only way she would be legally protected from his ongoing deceit. At sixty years old, Betty needed to figure out how she was going to support herself without becoming a burden on her adult children. Her husband was on his own and would need to live out the consequences of his deceit, theft, and lack of remorse.

When I'm working with someone considering divorce, my role as a coach or counselor is to listen carefully, to help clarify what's really going on, and to help a person get healthy and strong enough to make wise and biblical decisions on how she is going to handle her situation. Divorce is the last resort when efforts to reconcile and bring true peace in the marriage have repeatedly failed.

However, for some women, divorce might be the best choice because of her and her children's safety and sanity. I've already shared stories from women who wished they would not have stayed married for the children. They see their adult children living out the same destructive patterns that they witnessed as children. How they wish it could have been different.

Boiling It Down

In summary, if you stay, stay well. Get help for yourself so you don't have a breakdown. Distance yourself emotionally. Have no expectations. Connect with other women. Grow, learn, be as healthy and whole as you can while in a destructive marriage.

If you must leave, leave well. Expose his indifference, his verbal abuse, deceit, or whatever is destroying your marriage to your church leaders and separate for the purposes of reconciliation in the hopes that it will bring him to his senses. When you put your foot down and say, "I will not allow myself or the kids to be treated this way anymore. It's destructive to me, to them, and to our marriage," you are not going against God by speaking the truth in love. You are standing for goodness, for truth, and for the healing and restoration of your marriage. But now you refuse to pretend and stay together at any cost, including your own physical, emotional, mental, or spiritual health.

> *Dear God,*
>
> *I need a change of heart, because without one I don't know if I can trust you enough. I need to surrender my marriage to you. My children to you. My future to you. I am going to trust you and keep walking forward, knowing that you know what I have to live with. Show me what changes are necessary in order for our marriage to survive and be healed.*

Action Step: Where are you right now? If you're staying, are you staying well? What is something you can do to improve your own well-being? If you're separated, are you separated well? If not, what changes do you need to make?

Twelve

Necessary Changes for a Marriage to Heal

He who disdains instruction despises his own soul,
But he who heeds rebuke gets understanding.

—Proverbs 15:32, NKJV

Peter called again," my office manager texted me. "He's angry and wants to talk with you now."

Although I was away from the office, I gave Peter a call. He answered on the first ring. He didn't even say hello. "Leslie, I thought we were supposed to do marriage counseling together. How are we going to work on our marriage if Debbie and I aren't in counseling together?"

I had already explained to Peter why we weren't going to do joint counseling after his abusive incident, but Peter wasn't buying it. After our last marital counseling session, Peter slapped Debbie in an angry rage and threw her to the floor. Because of it, Debbie filed for a temporary protection from abuse order with the court, and Peter was no longer living at home.

On the phone now, Peter acknowledged his behavior was wrong but added that Debbie was being disrespectful to him, badgering him about money. Debbie's account differed. She said he went berserk when she asked him where the money was that was missing from his paycheck.

Debbie didn't want a divorce, and neither did Peter, but this latest incident scared her so much that she was not willing to live with him until he got help. Peter was willing to get help, but he demanded they go to counseling together, as a couple.

"She's not innocent in this," he railed to me over the phone. "I was wrong. I shouldn't have hurt her, but if you had to live with the constant criticism and badgering I do, you might have slapped her too."

"Are you telling me that in that moment your only choice was to hit her and throw her to the floor?"

There was a long pause on the other end. Finally Peter said, "No, I guess not, but you don't understand. We aren't going to get anywhere if we aren't in counseling together."

When I wouldn't give in, Peter switched tactics. He said, "Certainly as a Christian counselor you don't endorse a long separation. I need to be with my family. You know God hates divorce."

"I know," I said. "But, Peter, God hates how you treat your wife, and he wants you to learn how to love her, not control her."

Peter hung up. He chose to go elsewhere for counseling. After six sessions he persuaded his Christian counselor to cut back their sessions to once a month. Peter said he was healed and now it was time for Debbie to start marriage counseling with him.

Despite being court ordered to have no contact with her, Peter put flowers and handwritten cards in Debbie's car while she was at work. In them he wrote how much he loved her and missed her.

Debbie cried. She told me, "I always wanted him to do these things for me, but I don't trust him. I think he's doing this so that I won't extend the protection from abuse order when we go to court next week."

"Time will tell, Debbie," I said. "Let's see what happens after court next week. There is a world of difference between professing love and actually practicing it."

The judge extended Debbie's protection order for six more months. Peter was furious. "Look what you're doing to our family," Peter said to Debbie after the hearing. The cards and flowers stopped. His support money dwindled. Debbie was forced to threaten legal action if Peter wouldn't continue paying support for their children and housing expenses.

"Maybe I should have dropped the protection order and let him come home," Debbie lamented. "What if he has changed?"

HEALING A DESTRUCTIVE MARRIAGE

What does it take to heal a destructive D-minus marriage like Debbie and Peter's—or yours? How can you know whether or not someone is truly sorry or repentant? And what changes are essential in order to stop the same destructive patterns from continuing?

Words alone will never tell you what a person is like or what he is going to be like. Jesus tells us that someone's history and current actions show you what they are like (see Matthew 7:15–20). If your husband has agreed he needs to change, that's great. Action steps are required if you want the destruction in your marriage to stop. If your husband says he's repentant or wants to stop behaving in destructive ways, you can print out a version of this chapter, written just for him, at www.leslievernick.com/the-emotionally-destructive-marriage. Give it to him to read. You may want to print out a copy for his accountability partners and your pastor or counselor. There is also a video for your husband to watch at this same site.

I want you to understand that these changes are not necessary only for your husband. As you examine your part in the destructive patterns in your marriage, they may be helpful for you too. Hopefully you've already been doing some of these things as you've been reading this book.

If he is not willing, you can still do your own work, but your marriage cannot be repaired or restored until he agrees that he, too, needs to change.

Following are the changes you need to see if reconciliation is actually going to happen.

A Change of Heart

Peter's heart was sorrowful, but it was not a godly sorrow. He didn't feel sad or guilty over the pain he caused his wife and children by his violent outburst. Rather he felt bad about the pain he was in. He didn't like his consequences of having to live apart from his children or having to comply with the court order to stay away from his own house and wife. He told himself he was the victim of injustice…that the judge and I got it all wrong…that if only Debbie had been biblically submissive, then he would have never lost his temper. Peter's heart was not oriented around God or even his family, but just around himself. He misused the Bible to manipulate and intimidate others to get his way. Peter has no hope for change, and there is no healing of their marriage until he experiences and expresses a broken and contrite heart.[1]

Debbie wanted to know how she would be able to tell if Peter was truly sorry. We can't peer into someone's heart and see what is going on in there. But we can observe the results of repentance, which, if genuine, should become obvious in a person's outward demeanor, such as his words, attitude, and actions. Let's look at three outward indicators of an inward change of heart. The Bible calls these signs the fruit of repentance, and John the Baptist tells us to look for them as evidence that someone genuinely regrets the pain they caused both God and others (see Luke 3:8).

1. He Accepts Responsibility

One of the first things I look for to determine whether or not someone has experienced a change of heart is their willingness to see what they have done and take full responsibility for it. No blaming, rationalizing, lying, minimizing, or denying.

Peter saw that what he did was wrong, but he excused it by blaming Debbie. He dismissed the seriousness of his offense when he did not fully comply with the legal protection order and left cards and flowers in Debbie's car. He refused to consider that he had wrong ideas about biblical headship and submission, and unrealistic expectations of marriage and Debbie. He minimized his offenses while he maximized Debbie's. Peter shed many tears, but they weren't over the pain he caused Debbie. They were for the pain he felt over himself. Peter has obviously not had any inward change. He has a stubborn and hard heart, and in the Old Testament it sometimes led to divorce.[2]

Like Peter, Kevin came to counseling blaming his wife, Andrea, for his loss of control. Kevin would engage in verbal tirades and emotional battering whenever he felt angry or hurt. His words wounded Andrea every bit as much as Peter's slaps and physical abuse wounded Debbie. But over time, Kevin's eyes began to open, and he didn't like what he saw. He started to see his selfish demands and unrealistic expectations of Andrea. When he began to listen to his own words and voice tone, he saw how critical and sarcastic he became whenever Andrea voiced dissent or didn't want to do what he wanted or had her own ideas about things. He realized Andrea wasn't free to be Andrea if it didn't suit him.

After many months of personal counseling, Kevin stopped blaming Andrea as much and began taking responsibility for himself. He still got frustrated with her, but he also saw that she was not the primary cause of his pain or his sin. One evening after a tough counseling session, Kevin heaved a deep sigh and said, "I think I'm starting to get it. It's not okay for me to treat her that way."

Kevin knew that if he wanted a better marriage, it was up to him to change. He couldn't sow discord or spew toxic waste all over his wife and still expect to reap the benefits of a great marriage. It's impossible.

2. He Makes Amends

The second outward evidence of an inward change is a person's willingness to make amends to the one who has been harmed. In both the Old and New Testaments, making amends toward someone harmed by your sin was seen as evidence of true repentance.[3] For example, when Jesus singled out the chief tax collector, Zacchaeus, and invited himself to his home for lunch, something miraculous happened. Zacchaeus's eyes were opened and his heart was changed. He saw not only the loveliness and grace of Christ but also the ugliness of his greed, selfishness, and lack of love. As a tax collector, Zacchaeus made money extorting his own people, the Jews. The Bible describes him as a very wealthy man. But now, money was no longer Zacchaeus's first love; Jesus was. As a result, Zacchaeus said he would give half his wealth to the poor and would repay those he cheated fourfold. We know Zacchaeus had a change of heart because we can see it in his actions (see Luke 19:1–10).

Sometimes destructive individuals expect amnesty once they say they're sorry for what they've done. They believe that sorry means no more consequences, no extra effort, and that we shouldn't have to talk about it anymore. They believe their words of repentance automatically restore trust and repair relationship wounds. But words are not enough. Words can be deceptive (see Jeremiah 7:4). A heart that is changed shows it.[4]

For example, Corey and Adam were driving home from the movies when a speeding driver cut them off. Adam was furious. Screaming profanities out his window, Adam gunned the accelerator, racing to catch the offensive driver. He swerved in and out of lanes while Corey screamed, begging him to slow down. Adam lost control, and the car flew off the road and tumbled down a deep ditch. Adam escaped without injury, but Corey was not as fortunate. She suffered serious damage to her legs and pelvis. Six months later, she still walked with a cane.

One Sunday afternoon, Corey felt good enough to go for a ride to visit their grandkids, about an hour's drive away. It started to rain. Corey felt anxious and said, "Adam, could you please slow down?"

Adam was tempted to argue that she was overreacting and he wasn't driving that fast, but he stopped himself. He took Corey's hand as he slowed his speed. He said, "I don't ever want you to feel afraid when you're in the car with me. I am so sorry about what happened last year, and I will do whatever you need to feel safe."

Adam can't repair the damage to Corey's body, but genuine repentance demonstrates a willingness to endure consequences without complaint. If Corey is afraid when Adam drives, he needs to respect that and do what he can to help her trust him again. He is making amends for the damage he's caused to their relationship, not expecting amnesty.

3. He Displays Willingness Rather than Willfulness

The third evidence of a change of heart is an attitude of willingness instead of willfulness. The Bible describes people who are willful. They are foolish, rebellious, and evil, and they are always destructive. On the contrary, when a person's heart is changed, there is evidence that he has humbled himself before God and others. He can admit that he can't do it on his own, he is not always right, and some of the things he has done have been foolish and destructive. As a result, he is now willing to be taught new ways of handling his temper and disappointment. He is willing to surrender to God and submit to others in order to grow and become the man God calls him to be. He is willing to have others speak into his life and hold him accountable for the changes he knows he needs to make. Finally, he is willing to put in the necessary hard work to get there.

A change of heart is the first necessary step toward rebuilding a broken marriage, but it is not enough. Jesus warned his disciples that "the spirit indeed is willing, but the flesh is weak" (Matthew 26:41). Many of us are willing but not capable (yet) of doing what our minds and hearts desire. For example, I am willing to run a 10K race to raise money for breast cancer, but if the race were today, my body (flesh) would collapse in a heap about sixty-five seconds into the race. That doesn't mean I can't ever run a 10K, but I can't run one today. I need time to build my muscles and stamina so that my legs and my lungs can accomplish what my will wants them to. In addition, some mornings I find it hard to get out of bed and exercise. I don't feel like it, and it's tempting to give up my goal. It feels easier to pull the covers over my head and forget my commitment to run that race. To stay motivated and moving toward my goal, I need accountability partners who will challenge me, encourage me, and sometimes drag me out of bed when I get lazy, distracted, or discouraged.

God wants to help us change our destructive ways. He wants us to have healthy marriages, but it takes effort, particularly when your normal way of relating with someone has been so damaging. François Fénelon wrote, "A persuaded mind and even a well intentioned heart is a long way from exact and faithful practice."[5] The Bible says the same thing when Paul tells young Timothy, "Train yourself to be godly" (1 Timothy 4:7, NIV).

A Change in Habit

Admitting our destructive behaviors and repenting of them is the first step. Stopping them and acquiring godly attitudes and actions takes a lifetime. Christian maturity is a process. It's an inner orientation of where we're headed, not a once-and-done finished process. Change and growth requires time, effort, accountability to others, and perseverance. The Bible indicates this work is necessary for all believers because every one of us will have things we need to change. The Bible says,

> So put to death the sinful, earthly things lurking within you.
> Have nothing to do with sexual immorality, impurity, lust, and
> evil desires. Don't be greedy, for a greedy person is an idolater,
> worshiping the things of this world. Because of these sins, the
> anger of God is coming. You used to do these things when your
> life was still part of this world. *But now is the time to get rid of*
> *anger, rage, malicious behavior, slander, and dirty language. Don't*
> *lie to each other, for you have stripped off your old sinful nature and*
> *all its wicked deeds. Put on your new nature, and be renewed as*
> *you learn to know your Creator and become like him.* (Colossians
> 3:5–10, NLT)

The passage goes on to describe specific changes that we need to make if we want loving relationships. We must learn how to handle our disappointment, anger, and hurt in nondestructive ways. People will inevitably fail us or let us down, but abuse, deceit, or indifference doesn't have to be our response. We can learn to be wise and to love and forgive.

Kevin said, "Sometimes I feel overwhelmed with all I need to learn.

I never saw how critical and negative I was and how hard it is to change those habits. Sometimes my words are out of my mouth before I realize it."

"Don't let Satan discourage you," I said. "You're on the right track, but you aren't going to change everything all at once. Right now you're more aware of how harsh you've been with Andrea. Let's start with that."

Here are three things that will help in your husband's growth process. He may feel uncomfortable doing them at first because he will feel vulnerable. They require him to be honest with himself and others.[6] Facing the truth about ourselves hurts our egos and we feel shame. But remember, the pain of healthy shame keeps us moving toward our goal of godly change. When we refuse to feel it, we can't or won't make the necessary corrections to avoid personal and interpersonal disaster.

1. He Can Start to Keep a Journal

In chapter 5, I showed how critical self-awareness is for growth and maturity. We can't change something if we can't see it or won't look at it. Your husband has been blind and unwilling to see his own destructive behavior. If he wants to change it, he must learn to become more aware. The Bible tells us, "So be careful how you live. Don't live like fools, but like those who are wise" (Ephesians 5:15, NLT).

Each evening or morning (or both), he needs to reflect on four questions. In his answers he might want to differentiate between work time, church time, and home time, as he usually will not have the same responses in each setting. It's especially important that he learns to pay attention to himself when he's under stress. What are his physical warning bells that he's about to lose it? If he's not aware of the first signs, then he won't be able to take appropriate steps to deal with it constructively. He needs to ask himself:

1. *How did my body feel today?* Was he tense? relaxed? stressed? tired? irritable? hungry? anxious? What are his body's signals that he's getting worked up? Is he experiencing a headache? irritable bowel? pain in his neck? clenched fists? Is he able to put into words the sensations he's having in his body? If not, he needs help in learning how to understand his body's internal warning system.

2. *How did I treat people, particularly my spouse, today?* Was he respectful? detached? engaged? loving? deceitful? abusive? rude? sarcastic? shaming? If he treated you sinfully, did he take responsibility or blame-shift? Did he apologize? make amends? If not, why not?

3. *Were my actions today in line with the person I say I want to be?* For example, if he said he wanted to be a loving husband or a godly man, did he behave that way? If he said he wanted to be a man of integrity, was he honest today? If he said he wanted to be a man with a pure heart, was he lustful today? If he said he wanted to be a good steward of his body, did he stick to his diet? drink too much alcohol? do other things with his body that he would not want to tell you?

4. *In what nonsexual ways did I show my spouse that she's important to me and I care about her today?* Did he help you with the children? call or text you from work to let you know he was thinking about you? stop and pick up something at the grocery store without complaining? give you a nonsexual hug or kiss with no expectations for later? bring home flowers?

Daily asking himself these four questions and answering them will help him start to notice unhealthy patterns and ways he becomes triggered to react in negative ways. Writing down his thoughts and feelings helps him see where his thinking may be unrealistic, entitled, and self-centered. Learning to examine himself and reflect upon his thoughts, feelings, and behaviors keeps him mindful that he still has a long way to go and is not all better yet. This is good to know so he doesn't think he has it all together, stop growing, and revert back to his old ways.

2. He Must Receive Feedback

When we want to learn something new or difficult, we do best when we have people in our lives who regularly gives us feedback on our progress, or lack thereof. When we were in school, tests were feedback to let us know whether or not we learned the material.

When my daughter took piano lessons, each week her teacher gave her something new and pointed out the things she needed to work on. Some weeks her fingers were in the wrong position; other times she was playing the wrong notes or her timing was off. Without weekly feedback, she would not have made corrections, she would have developed bad habits, and she wouldn't have made much progress in her piano playing.

But feedback isn't just for beginners or students. Everyone needs feedback. For example, every day I invite my scale to give me feedback on whether or not I'm eating too much. Top athletes, musicians, and high-level CEOs hire coaches to help them see what they can't see. We all have blind spots, and wise people know that asking for and receiving feedback from trusted others helps us grow and be our best. Proverbs says, "Wise words bring many benefits, and hard work brings rewards" (Proverbs 12:14, NLT).

One of my coaching clients recently asked her husband what he would like her to do when he has hurt her. He answered, "I don't care, but don't tell me."

"Now what?" she said. "I don't know how to do a relationship this way. There is no resolution to the problem, no working it out, no change if I'm not allowed to give him feedback when he hurts me."

Sadly, her husband preferred to stay blind. He didn't want to know. If his zipper was down or his face was smudged with dirt, wouldn't he want to know even if it embarrassed him? In the same way, your spouse needs to be willing to hear feedback from you about how his actions impact you. If he thinks he handled himself wisely and you give him feedback that he was harsh, he'd best pay attention if he sincerely wants to change his habit of being harsh.[7]

3. He Can Join a Small Group of Believers and Invite Accountability

We were never designed to mature or grow up all by ourselves. God places children into families where he instructs parents to train their children in good character qualities and important life skills. Sadly, many of us have not received godly training from our biological families. The good news is it's never too late to learn.

God gives all of us opportunities for continued lessons in character building and interpersonal skills so that we can heal, change, and grow. He puts us into the family of God where we can unlearn sinful and destructive ways and learn new ways of living and loving and expressing ourselves with others.

Recently, I received an e-mail from a man whose wife accused him of being controlling and domineering, always having to be right and have the final word. He disagreed with her assessment of him. He said he simply wanted to discuss things and thought she was avoiding constructive problem solving. Who is right? I encouraged him to humbly invite feedback from work colleagues, his grown children, and other people who know him well and see if they ever feel the same way his wife does. After he asked them, he was embarrassed to find out that everyone also saw him as pushy and controlling. He didn't see it. For his growth, I advised him to join a small group, share that he has a problem with validating other people's points of view, and ask them to help him learn to listen and not always push for his own way even when he believes he's right. This will help him stay aware of this tendency as well as change it.

Alcoholics Anonymous began transforming the lives of alcoholics with a twelve-step program for change. It was birthed in the conviction that an alcoholic was helpless to stop drinking all by himself. He needed God (or "a higher power" as it's now referred to) and others to walk alongside him in the healing journey. In one of their books, it says, "Almost none of us liked the self-searching, the leveling of our pride, the confession of shortcomings which the process requires for its successful consummation. But we saw that it really worked in others, and we had come to believe in the hopelessness and futility of life as we had been living it."[8]

A small group of supportive individuals helps us make those necessary changes. It's much harder to hide and stay self-deceived when we've invited other people to give us feedback and hold us accountable to the goals we've set.

4. He Can't Stop Growing

Every human being is in the process of becoming. We are either becoming more like Christ or more like the world, more loving or more self-centered. The direction we head is up to us, but we have to have our eyes open and our hearts humble. The apostle Paul said, "I don't mean to say that I have already achieved these things or that I have already reached perfection. But I press on to possess that perfection for which Christ Jesus first possessed me. No, dear brothers and sisters, I have not achieved it, but I focus on this one thing: Forgetting the past and looking forward to what lies ahead, I press on to reach the end of the race and receive the heavenly prize for which God, through Christ Jesus, is calling us" (Philippians 3:12–14, NLT).

We all have necessary changes to make to become the person God calls us to be. When we're open, teachable, and willing, the Holy Spirit has fertile ground in which to build Christlike character qualities in our lives, and this leads to great relationships. A change of heart and habit is for all of us who love God and want to grow. Even if your husband isn't willing, I hope you continue to press on.

> ### Dear God,
>
> *I see how these changes would benefit my husband and my marriage. They are part of your plan to mature us and help us live holy, healthy, and happy lives. God, I want a change of heart and a change of habit. Please help my husband to want them too.*

Action Step: Read Philippians 2:19–22. Notice Paul's confidence in young Timothy. What did Timothy possess that gave Paul that kind of confidence? Character is much more important than charm in loving relationships. What is one thing in your attitudes or actions that you can intentionally work on in your own life to build a track record of proven character?

Thirteen

Restoring the Destructive Marriage

Do not hide your darkness; expose it. Do not sympathetically make excuses for it; confess it. Hate it. Renounce it. For as long as darkness remains in darkness, it rules you. But when you bring darkness out into the light, it becomes light. When you take your secret sins and boldly come unto the throne of God's grace and confess them, He cleanses you from all unrighteousness.

—Francis Frangipane

I don't know where to go from here," Charlotte said. "He seems repentant. I see some changes, but how do I know they will last? We need a road map. What does it take to put this marriage back together in a healthy way? And if we don't or can't, then what? Do we stay legally together even if we're relationally divorced? What does God want us to do?"

I get asked many versions of the same question each week from men and women in deeply troubled and destructive marriages. Some of them have sought professional counseling, others church or pastoral help—most with little success or lasting change. Sometimes the patterns are never addressed at all. Instead, they receive biblical instruction about the roles of husbands and wives, or are taught communication skills or conflict management techniques, or receive encouragement to have more date nights or try harder to be more loving or submissive. But the deeper root issues and destructive patterns never get talked through, changed, or healed.

Why is that? Does God not give us a means for healing damaged relationships? He does, but his blueprint is not unilateral. Healing a destructive marriage can never be the sole responsibility of one person in the relationship. It always takes two people willing to work to achieve godly change. There needs to be forgiveness sought and forgiveness granted. There need to be amends made and a willingness to rebuild trust. There needs to be constructive feedback given and willingly received. When one person refuses to participate or take responsibility for his or her part, healing or restoration of the relationship cannot fully take place.

Healing a destructive marriage can never be the sole responsibility of one person in the relationship. It always takes two people willing to work to achieve godly change.

Throughout this book I've talked about various types of destructive relationships. They all require a change of heart and a commitment to work toward a change of habit to bring about restoration. No one goes through these two processes all at once or perfectly, so I want to give you a few mile markers that will help you identify where you are on the healing journey or whether or not you're even on the right path toward getting there.

Safety

We've talked about the importance of safety throughout this book, but it bears repeating. You cannot put a marriage together in a healthy way if one person in the marriage feels afraid of the other. Without question, whenever there has been any kind of physical abuse, destruction of property, or threats against one's self or others, there is no safety.

Shirley e-mailed me. She said, "My counselor says that I must allow my husband back into the home if we want our marriage to heal. He said, 'How can you work on your marriage when you're not living together?'"

"What are your concerns about him moving back home?" I asked.

"We've been separated for over a year, after he gave me a black eye. It wasn't the first time he hit me, but it was the worst. I never pressed charges or called the police, but I told him he'd have to move out. Honestly, I haven't seen any real change in him. My counselor says he sees Ray changing. He hasn't hit me for a long time. I agreed, but his disrespect and underlying attitudes of entitlement and bullying behaviors are still there."

"Give me a few examples," I said.

"He badgers me to give in to him, and when I disagree, he starts verbally assaulting me. For example, when he visits the kids at the house, sometimes it gets late. When I tell him I'm tired and I want him to leave, he says I'm selfish and only thinking about myself. He thinks it's okay if he walks into our house without knocking, even though I've asked him not to. If he won't respect my boundaries when we're separated, how will he do it if he moves back home?"

"He won't," I said. "Either he's not willing to respect your boundaries or he's not capable of doing it, but either way you are not safe until he learns to do this. Please stick up for yourself with your counselor. Before you can work on the marriage, your husband needs to respect your right to say no to him, demonstrate that he can control himself when he's upset with you, and honor your boundaries. If he won't do this much, you cannot go any further to repair your relationship."

There are other issues of safety that also must be resolved to some degree if a marriage is going to be wisely restored. For example, Kathy still loves her husband despite his sins against her. She longs for Jeff to be the man she knows he could be. Yet she must not throw caution to the side and be fully reconciled with Jeff without the proper safety measures in place. She knows Jeff has a problem with sexual addiction. He has a long history of pornography, affairs, prostitutes, and one-night stands.

Does God ask Kathy to ignore these dangers to her health and safety in order to reconcile her marriage? Or is it both in her and Jeff's best interests that she stay firm and not have sexual intimacy with Jeff until he gets a clean bill of health and demonstrates a change of heart and some progress in his change of habits?

In another situation, Matthew feels entitled to keep his income separate from the family income. He contributes a set amount, which he's determined, into their joint bank account each time he is paid, but the rest he keeps in his own account with only his name on it. Gina is a registered nurse, but she and Matthew agreed it was best for her to stay home right now and homeschool their four children. Gina does not feel safe financially or emotionally. She feels like a child when she has to give an account of the money she spent, yet Matthew refuses to let Gina know what he's spending or even what he earns. He says it's his money. Gina feels vulnerable and scared whenever Matthew travels, especially overseas. What if something happened to him and she ran out of cash? How would she feed the children? When she's expressed her concerns to Matthew, he tells her not to worry, that nothing will happen to him. Gina's not allowed to have a credit card for emergencies.

Legally, Gina is an adult and considered an equal partner in their financial responsibilities, yet she has no voice, no power, and no idea what is happening with their assets. Should she submit to Matthew when he says she's not allowed to have a credit card, even though she's never been irresponsible with money? Gina's observed Matthew being deceitful at times in claiming his business expenses. What if Matthew has been deceitful in other ways? For example, what if he chooses not to pay their taxes? Gina would be held equally responsible, even if she didn't know. What if he is not paying their mortgage or their home-equity loan? The financial consequences of his irresponsibility would fall equally on her shoulders. Gina and Matthew will never have a healthy marriage if these issues aren't discussed with the underlying imbalance of power and control changed.

> There can be no constructive conversation about other marital issues if one person has no say or isn't safe to tell the truth or disagree without fear of physical, emotional, sexual, financial, or spiritual retaliation.

Safety always comes first when restoring a destructive marriage. There can be no constructive conversation about other marital issues if one person has no say or isn't safe to tell the truth or disagree without fear of physical, emotional, sexual, financial, or spiritual retaliation.

SANITY

We've already learned that thinking truthfully is a high value to God. Living truthfully is equally important. When we habitually pretend, placate, deny reality, lie to ourselves and others, we become more troubled and destructive (see Romans 1:25–32). The hardest lies to discern are those that sound true, especially when they're disguised as God's truth.

If a destructive marriage is to be healed, you and your husband must become aware of the lies you both believe. I've already covered many of the lies a woman in a destructive marriage must refute if she wants to get healthy. Here are some common lies I've identified in the men I've worked with:

- God says I'm the head of my home; therefore, she has to do what I say.
- God says I'm the head of my home; therefore, I get to make all the decisions my way.
- God says a woman is to obey her husband.
- I deserve more.
- God says she should forgive me and never bring it up again.
- I can't change; this is just the way I am.
- If my wife makes me mad, it's her own fault if I lose my temper on her.
- I can't control myself. If I get mad enough, I will flip out.
- It's not abusive to smash things; I'm just venting.
- If she's hurt by what I say (or do), that's her problem.
- She deserved it. She asks to be hit.
- She gives me no choice (to lie, to hit, to watch pornography, to curse).
- God says a woman's role is to serve the man.
- It's not my fault (or responsibility).
- A husband has the right to tell a wife what she can do or where she can go.
- What I do is none of her business.
- What I earn is mine.
- She is being contentious or a nag when she asks me questions or tries to hold me accountable.

- She is not carrying her weight financially. She just sees me as a paycheck.
- The Bible says I have the right to have sex with my wife whenever I want to.
- The Bible says she has no right to say no to me.
- If she hurts me, I have every right to hurt her back.
- She should always put me first.
- If she loves me, she'd do what I want.
- If she respects me, she won't disagree or challenge my decisions.
- She should always respect me and do what I want without arguing.
- She should stop doing things that upset me.
- I have the right to be in control of my home and my wife.
- She should do it my way. God says that's the way he designed marriage to work.
- She makes a big deal out of nothing.
- I'll never please her.
- The past is the past, and she shouldn't bring it up anymore.

Any of these sound familiar? Before you can work together on solving marital problems, these untruths must be uprooted, exposed as lies, and refuted. This is usually done in individual counseling, not marital work. If they are not recognized, challenged, and changed, these lies continue to be the foundation of your husband's thinking and, therefore, his problem-solving strategies. There is no possibility of working together to build a healthy relationship if you both aren't free to talk, to question, to disagree, or to hold someone accountable for the commitments they've made. The Bible says that one of the main steps we all need to take in order to grow and change is to renew our minds (see Romans 12:2).

Therefore, a husband and wife together, and separately, must be committed to truth seeking and truth telling if restoration is to take place.

Remember, sanity for you requires you to give up your fantasy of what you wished your marriage was like and face what it is really like. Sanity requires you to stop trying harder to do the same things that haven't worked and understand what your biblical role is as your husband's helpmate. You need to learn how to execute godly thinking and live from your CORE so that you won't retaliate in anger and become abusive yourself. Sanity keeps you centered in God and not in having a good marriage or loving husband. It also helps you protect yourself and get safe (see Proverbs 27:12).

Sanity for your husband means that he must take the time to examine his unrealistic expectations of marriage and of women, and expose his underlying attitudes of entitlement. He must come to understand the truth. There is no perfect wife or marriage. He must come to value his wife as a separate person, not an object. She has her own thoughts, feelings, dreams, and needs. She can't and won't meet his every need or always revolve herself around his wants. He needs to recognize the lie he tells himself that he's entitled to the perks of married life no matter how he treats you. Or that he shouldn't have to experience negative consequences as a result of his behavior, or that forgiveness means automatic restoration with no consequences, no amends, or no work. Sanity means he must learn to take responsibility for his own thoughts and his own behaviors without blaming others. He must also learn to handle his emotions, such as disappointment, frustration, anger, and hurt, in new ways that don't damage people, things, or relationships. If he wants to have a good relationship with his wife, sanity means that he now understands he needs to take responsibility for his part and do the work to make that happen.

Once a man has completed the sanity stage, a husband and wife can begin to work as a couple to build a new history together because he has accepted the five Cs of change:

Clarity: He sees that he has been destructive, abusive, indifferent, deceitful, controlling toward his partner, and he no longer wants to behave in those ways.

Commitment: He is willing to be accountable and teachable in order to grow and become the person he wants to become. If there is any question of safety violation, he will immediately call his supportive community and temporarily remove himself from the situation or the home when needed.

Community: He will allow others, including his wife, to speak into his life. He will listen and prayerfully consider what the community has to say about his attitudes and behaviors.

Confession: He will own his wrongdoing instead of blaming, minimizing, or rationalizing it. He will confess his sin to God and to the person he's hurt. If he violates this agreement or engages in abusive tactics, such as bullying, intimidating, withdrawing, for longer than twenty-four hours without consultation from his support team, or does other behaviors that frighten his spouse, he understands that restoration of the marriage is not possible at this time.

Consequences: He humbly accepts the consequences of his sin and makes restitution where needed to restore the relationship.

STABILITY

Creating a healthy relationship out of the broken pieces of the destructive one takes courage and time. It requires building a new history together that contains mutuality, reciprocity, and freedom. That is only possible once safety is established and sanity is well underway. When a physical separation is in place, there needs to be concrete evidence demonstrating safety and sanity before a couple can move back in together. The last thing you want is to start repeating the same old patterns of abuse and destruction that caused the split in the first place. You can't build new history together when the old history keeps repeating itself.

Remember the story at the beginning of the chapter about Shirley's concern around her Christian counselor's mandate that she allow Ray to move back home? He said that they could not put the marriage together while still separated. Shirley's fear was that she hadn't seen enough evidence of Ray respecting her boundaries while separated. That repeats their old history of Ray's needs always coming first. Ray gets what Ray wants. Ray feels entitled to badger and bully to get what he wants. Shirley is not allowed to say no.

We know Ray isn't going to be perfect. Change doesn't happen overnight. But Ray could be working on building new history with Shirley, even while separated. For example, if Ray is working on sanity and safety goals, then he must start to see his self-centered orientation. He also must accept Shirley's feedback when she sees he's repeating old patterns. Let's see what this looks like:

"Ray, I want you to leave now. I'm tired. The kids are tired. We all want to go to bed," Shirley says. *(Shirley is asking Ray to be considerate of her needs.)*

"This is my house too. I don't know why I can't stay and finish watching the football game. Go to bed. I don't care." *(Ray is only thinking about Ray.)*

"Ray, I'm not comfortable going to sleep with you in the house. Please leave." *(Shirley is being honest and asking for respect.)*

"You're being selfish. Don't you know how boring it is in that room I have to stay in because of you? All I ask is to finish watching the game. It will be over in thirty minutes. Go to bed or stay up, but I want to see who wins." *(Ray is attacking and blame shifting. He is still in his old patterns. He is not practicing safety or sanity.)*

"You are not respecting my boundaries. It's not because of me that you are not living in this house; it is because of your own abusive actions. Right now you're behaving like your wants come before everyone else's. I said I was tired, and I want you to leave." *(Shirley is giving Ray feedback on his words and behavior. This gives him an opportunity to stop in that moment and reflect about what he's saying and doing and decide which Ray he wants to be. Is he going to be old Ray who continues to selfishly demand his own way and expects everyone to cater to him? Or is he going to build new history by caring that Shirley is tired, respecting her boundary, and going home? If he capitulates to Shirley's request and goes home, is he going to handle his disappointment in not being able to watch the end of the game in a godly way, or is he going to retaliate by slamming the door, calling her names, or other abusive behaviors? If so, old history is repeated. If not, new history is beginning.)* This type of interaction becomes exhausting when it repeats itself over and over again with no change.

Last week I was talking with a couple who have been building new history together. Their old history is that he's been extremely critical, demeaning, and unappreciative of Wendy, a stay-at-home mom. He now sees how destructive that's been, and he doesn't want to do that anymore, but old habits die hard. Recently they celebrated a small victory. John came home, tired and crabby, fighting a cold and sore throat. Dinner wasn't ready, and he started in on Wendy. "What have you been doing all day?" he snarled.

Wendy started to defend herself, but before she got the words out of her mouth, John said, "I'm sorry. You don't deserve that. I know you work hard all day around here." Then he walked over and gave her a hug.

Wendy felt encouraged. She didn't have to remind him not to talk to her that way. John reminded himself and self-corrected before it got worse. He apologized for his demeaning tone and words and affirmed her value. He also didn't minimize it or make excuses for his bad behavior because he wasn't feeling well. These small and seemingly insignificant moments of stopping old patterns and creating new ones, repeated again and again, start to build a new marital history. Seeing evidence of these changes creates confidence that even when old history rears its ugly head, it won't stay long. The old patterns are recognized and stopped so that more damage doesn't occur. Seeds of trust are planted that build hope that the process of restoration is happening.

Creating stability in the aftermath of a destructive marriage is about rebuilding shattered trust. We want to see evidence of *Do you hear me? Can you respect me? Do you follow through on your promises? Do you care about how I feel? Can you take responsibility for yourself when you mess up? Can I count on you to control your temper? Can I trust you to tell me the truth? Can I trust you to tell yourself the truth? Will you be accountable?*

Marriage counseling can be helpful in this stage to help the couple learn healthy communication skills and develop godly ways to resolve conflict and talk through old hurts in a constructive way. When there is no safety and no sanity, joint counseling is ineffective and often danger-ous. If he can't see his part or take responsibility for his own wrong think-ing, beliefs, or attitudes, everything ends up being blamed on you. Old history keeps repeating itself, even in the counselor's office.

> Just like it wasn't possible for you to fix everything
> when his heart was hard and he was unwilling,
> it's not possible for him to fix everything either.

Perhaps it's hard for you to ever imagine you and your husband mak-ing new history together. In the meantime, I want to encourage you to pay attention to what's happening to you and in you. As you wake up and see all the destruction you've endured, you might feel furious. You've felt so misunderstood, so misjudged, so wounded, and so unprotected—not only by your husband but often by your church family, friends, and loved ones. Now finally someone hears you. You feel validated. Someone gets what you've lived with for the last twenty-seven years.

Your anger is valid, but be cautious. Feel it and use it wisely to help you get strong and protect yourself and your children. Use it to speak up for yourself and stand up to injustice, abuse, and misuse of power and privilege. But don't let it deceive you into thinking that you have no work to do if you want your marriage restored. Someone once said it takes two to make a marriage, but only one to destroy it. Sometimes when I see a husband get to the stage of being capable and willing to rebuild his marriage, his wife is unwilling. She's exhausted and has lost her compassion. She's allowed her anger to harden into resentment and believes that it's now his responsibility to fix everything if their marriage is going to be healed. But that's not true. Just like it wasn't possible for you to fix everything when his heart was hard and he was unwilling, it's not possible for him to fix everything either. Each of you must ask God to open your eyes to see what's going on in your own heart and habits. Ask God to give you humility and wisdom so that he can take a marriage that was ugly and broken and create something beautiful for you, for your husband, children, and grandchildren, and ultimately, for his glory.

SECURITY

God designed marriage to be a safe haven—a place where a husband and wife can be naked together and unashamed. A place where we can be at our most vulnerable and know we will be loved, accepted, and respected without fear that we will be intentionally harmed by the ones closest to us.

Sin damaged God's design. Sin always damages relationships. But

God's plan for our salvation and restoration is not just for when we get to heaven someday, but for now. When we are in Christ, he tells us that we are a new creation. We are to be changed and restored. We could never do it on our own, but with his power and wisdom and strength, we can participate in a miracle.

> ### Dear God,
>
> *Give me wisdom and discernment. If my husband is willing to do this work, help me walk out my part of the restoration process, holding your hand, clinging to your truth, trusting in your help. Help me forgive as you forgive me. Help me love as you love me.*

Action Step: What step could you take to more fully cooperate in the restoration process, if it is indeed happening?

Epilogue

I hope you are no longer hanging on by a thread but have grabbed hold of the lifeline of grace and truth God offers you. I hope you are no longer isolated but have surrounded yourself with supportive individuals who will help you through your suffering. I hope you no longer see God as against divorce, but for the genuine healing of your marriage.

If your marriage is being restored, I'd love to hear about it. What an opportunity you and your husband have to demonstrate hope to other broken couples through your story of what God is doing. There is so much secrecy and shame surrounding destructive marriages in the church that it's very difficult for both a husband and wife to receive the support and help they both desperately need in order to heal the damage.

In closing, I thought it would encourage you to hear how one man is learning how to be a better man. He is working hard. He still doesn't always get it or treat his wife well, but he now sees it more than he ever has. But he can't do it alone. He's in individual counseling and attending a group for abusive men, and I've asked him to share how crucial his church family is to his continued progress. These are his words:

> David sat across from me, silent, as I continued to stare at the keys on the conference table. I can't recall anything in particular I was thinking at the time; I'm not even sure I was thinking at all. He

had just urged me to use his guesthouse, which he maintains for family and friends and for missionaries on furlough. Later, David would tell me that I sat staring at the keys for forty-two minutes. Thus began my two weeks out of the house after I had committed an incident of abuse—not the only one in my history, but perhaps the proverbial straw on the camel's back—that left my wife more desperate and fearful than ever before.

Those forty-two minutes, when David sat with me without words, patiently loving me, are perhaps a snapshot in time of how he—and my church—have walked with me and my family over the last several years. David has been both gentle and patient, stern and urgent, as he has alternately encouraged me, admonished me, rebuked me, and exhorted me. Always with Christ's fierce strength, always pointing me back to Christ.

Over the last year or so, David has also been coming with me to my counseling sessions with Leslie. Extraordinary? I'm sure it is. But *I* believe that his presence in these sessions has been invaluable. Sometimes when I say something to Leslie, David is able to say, "Actually, do you remember…" to help me frame reality. At other times, he can say, "As Leslie just said…" or "In addition to what Leslie just said…" better to inform or to nuance her counsel. And when David and I meet weekly and I start drifting again, he can often say, "Do you remember what Leslie said the last time about that?"

I wish I could say that all this is now history, but it's not. I'm not where I was, but I'm not where I'd like to be. My family is not where it was, but it's not where I'd like it to be. I do know that without David, my extraordinary friend and elder, shepherding me with the authority of my church and walking beside me, we would not be where we are. I shudder to think where we *might* be.

I also know that my time with Leslie will come to an end at some point in time. But David and our church will continue to love me and my family long after that time. And God willing, we will pay it forward with others who wouldn't make it alone.

It's clear from Scripture that God is on the side of the oppressed. He cares for the victim and the helpless and calls his church to do likewise. Don't be afraid to let the people of God into your messy marriage. They are called by God to model a loving family to those who never had such an example, as well as model justice and protection when one of its members is destructive and unrepentant. Just like you, they aren't perfect, but together we can work to bring hope and healing to hurting people and shattered families.

Resources for Help

IMMEDIATE HELP

National Domestic Violence Hotline, www.thehotline.org or 1-800-799-7233 (or 1-800-787-3224 for TTY): Call for help in a crisis, or for assistance in developing a safety plan. Staffed 24 hours a day, 365 days a year.

Family Renewal Shelter, www.domesticviolencehelp.com or 1-253-475-9010 (24-hour crisis line) or 1-888-550-3915 (toll free): A Christian resource that provides crisis help and assistance developing a safety plan.

For an example of safety planning see www.theraveproject.com/index .php/resources/resource_content/personalized_safety_plan or www .overcomingpowerlessness.com/safety_plan.htm.

To find professional Christian counselors experienced in domestic violence, call Focus on the Family Counselors, 1-800-232-6459 (toll free), visit http://family.custhelp.com/app/home (find a counselor), or go to the American Association of Christian Counselors at AACC.net.

SUPPORT RESOURCES

Document the Abuse, www.documenttheabuse.com: Assists women who fear for their safety in developing an Evidentiary Abuse Affidavit (EAA) that combines videotaping of the victim's actual words attesting to the abuse, coupled with creative witnessed and notarized legal documents that successfully satisfy legal hurdles often faced in these intimate partner violence and stalking cases. The victim then has documented "testimony" to be used to press charges if she goes missing or something happens to her.

Family Renewal Shelter, www.familyrenewalshelter.com: A program based in Tacoma, WA, offering healing hope and new life to victims of domestic violence.

Women's Law, www.womenslaw.org: Offers state-specific legal information and resources for survivors of domestic violence, including information on how to gather evidence of abuse and prepare for court.

VINE (Victim Information and Notification Everyday), www.vinelink.com: Allows crime victims to obtain timely and reliable information about criminal cases and the custody status of offenders. It offers the ability to search for an offender by name or ID number and then register to be alerted if the offender has been released or has escaped. Available 24 hours a day in 47 states.

Lighthouse Network, www.lighthousenetwork.org or 1-877-562-2565: Assists individuals and their loved ones in finding effective treatment for drug, alcohol, psychological, or emotional struggles. Available 24 hours a day, 7 days a week.

EDUCATIONAL RESOURCES

www.leslievernick.com/the-emotionally-destructive-marriage: Free resource page with short video clips, podcasts, and other articles.

www.bradhambrick.com/selfcenteredspouse: Visit to read a great series of blogs by Brad Hambrick on the chronically self-centered spouse.

www.cryingoutforjustice.wordpress.com, a blog that addresses the needs of the evangelical church to recognize and validate the reality of abuse in the Christian home.

Humanity Against Local Terrorism (HALT), www.haltnow.ca: Dedicated to finding solutions to bullying, domestic violence, and terrorism.

No Safe Place, www.pbs.org/kued/nosafeplace: Documentary offering a thoughtful examination of the origins of violence against women, looking at the biological, sociological, cultural, and historical factors involved.

The Rave Project, www.theraveproject.com: Information, videos, and training for victims and church leaders to learn more about the impact of abuse.

FOCUS Ministries, www.focusministries1.org: Offers hope, encouragement, support, education, spiritual direction, and assistance to teens, women, and families who experience domestic violence, destructive relationships, separation, or divorce. They also have a ministry specific to pastors' wives.

Men Stopping Violence, www.menstoppingviolence.org: Works locally, nationally, and internationally to dismantle belief systems, social structures, and institutional practices that oppress women and children and dehumanize men themselves.

Futures Without Violence www.futureswithoutviolence.org: Works to prevent and end violence against women and children around the world.

MenEngage Global Alliance, www.menengage.org: Dedicated to engaging men and boys to end violence against women, and to questioning or challenging violent versions of manhood.

Safety Net Project, http://nnedv.org/projects/safetynet.html: Educates victims of stalking, domestic and sexual violence, their advocates, and the general public on strategic ways to use technology to help escape abusive relationships and situations. The Safety Net Project also trains police officers and prosecutors how to identify and hold perpetrators accountable for misusing technology.

God's Protection of Women: When Abuse Is Worse Than Divorce (Grand Rapids, MI: RBC Ministries, 2005), free to download, http://web001.rbc.org/pdf/discovery-series/gods-protection-of -women.pdf.

When Love Goes Wrong: What to Do When You Can't Do Anything Right; Strategies for Women with Controlling Partners by Ann Jones and Susan Schechter (New York: HarperPerennial, 1993). This book gives specific steps in developing a safety plan, how to protect your children, finding a safe place to stay if you plan to leave, and dealing with the police and legal system.

A Cry for Justice: How the Evil of Domestic Abuse Hides in Your Church by Jeff Crippen and Anna Wood (Calvary Press, 2012). This book is for church leaders to understand the church's role in wisely handling cases of marital and other kinds of abuse.

When Dad Hurts Mom: Helping Your Children Heal the Wounds of Witnessing Abuse by Lundy Bancroft (New York: Berkley, 2005). This book is an important resource in understanding the impact of destructive marriages on children and how to help them through it.

Mending the Soul: Understanding and Healing Abuse by Steven R. Tracy (Grand Rapids, MI: Zondervan, 2005). This book is a significant resource for those who have been victims of abuse and injustice at the hands of others, especially those who were family members. Tracy validates the long-term effects of abuse on one's personhood and provides a sound and biblical way for healing the wounds of the soul.

OTHER RESOURCES

Restore Relationships Counseling, www.restorerelationships.org:
Located in McKinney, TX.

Face to Face, www.facetofacesurgery.org or 1-800-842-4546: Provides
free plastic and reconstructive surgery for domestic violence victims
who have injuries to face, head, or neck.

Give Back a Smile, 1-800-773-4227: Provides free repair of front teeth
damaged by a violent partner or spouse.

Give Her Wings, www.giveherwings.com, a fund-raising ministry for
mothers who have left abusive situations.

SAMPLING OF TREATMENT GROUPS
FOR ABUSIVE SPOUSES

Domestic Abuse Intervention Programs, www.theduluthmodel.org or
1-218-722-2781: Offers an ever-evolving way of thinking about how
a community works together to end domestic violence.

Changing Men, Changing Lives, www.ChangingMenChangingLives
.org: A Christian version of the Domestic Abuse Intervention
Program.

RAVEN, www.ravenstl.org/dev: St. Louis program providing high-
quality domestic violence intervention and prevention services to
those at risk to commit violence.

Emerge, www.emergedv.com: Boston program seeking to educate
individual abusers, prevent young people from learning to accept
violence in their relationships, improve institutional responses to
domestic violence, and increase public awareness about the causes
and solutions to partner violence.

Manalive, www.mavcenter.org: California program committed to helping men age sixteen and older stop violence to themselves, their intimate partners, their families, and their communities.

Menergy, www.menergy.org: Philadelphia program for people who have been abusive to their intimate partners.

Five Common Mistakes People Helpers Make

If you are a counselor, coach, pastor, or marriage mentor working with destructive couples, there are some particular pitfalls that are crucial to avoid if you want to maximize the possibility of healing and minimize further damage. For more information on each of these five mistakes, please go to my free resource page at www.leslievernick.com/the-emotionally-destructive-marriage and watch the video *Five Common Mistakes People Helpers Make.*

1. Making the Wrong Diagnosis or Implementing the Wrong Treatment Plan

When my mother became ill with a nagging cough, her doctor diagnosed it as bronchitis and prescribed antibiotics. Week after week she made no improvement. He changed antibiotics a few times and added an inhaler for asthma. She got worse. It was only after an emergency trip to the hospital that we discovered that she did not have bronchitis after all; she had lung cancer.

If you are working with a couple, and despite your best efforts, they are getting sicker and sicker, it's time to reevaluate the diagnosis. Antibiotics are great for someone with bronchitis but impotent to treat cancer. In the same way, traditional Christian marriage counseling or coaching is impotent to tackle the problem of a couple who have a cancerous marriage, and it may actually make things worse. Review chapters 1–4 to understand the dynamics and destructive patterns of this type of relationship. Joint counseling is never appropriate if there are safety concerns.

2. Encouraging the Wife to Try Harder

As we've already seen in chapter 6, the reason this doesn't work is that it colludes with the husband's delusion that he's entitled to a fantasy wife, and it continues to foster the lie that she is responsible for his moods, attitudes, emotions, and behavior. A wife is often the first person to seek our help. If her husband joins her, he is usually there to hear what she's going to say about him, not because he sees himself as part of the problem. When we focus on her wrongdoing (which isn't difficult to find if you're looking for it), this reinforces her husband's misbelief that if only she would change, he would be fine and everything would be better.

3. Not Prioritizing Safety and Sanity

We (as the professional or helper) and our client can sometimes be so against divorce and separation and so anxious for restoration and reconciliation that we all collude to collapse the required steps necessary for genuine healing to take place. It's important that we not minimize the work during the safety and sanity stages, since these stages lay the foundation for genuine healing. These first two stages typically last a minimum of six months and at times much longer, even with weekly care.

Whenever a doctor diagnoses a patient with cancer, he or she recommends a treatment protocol that provides the best possible outcome. If the patient disagrees with what the doctor recommends or prefers to receive chemotherapy only once a month instead of weekly, the doctor would inform the patient that the treatment protocol calls for weekly chemotherapy and that less than that will not tackle the cancer. In the same way, we must be firm on what's required to restore broken and destructive marriages. Compromising the plan for restoration gives false hope.

4. Becoming a Benevolent Rescuer

There are times as people helpers we fear for a woman's safety and sanity. She seems perpetually stuck and incapable of acting wisely on her own behalf. In those moments, it is tempting to take charge and tell her what she must do. This is a mistake. Our role is not to fix or rescue her but rather to teach her how to make wise choices for her and her children. If she's been married to a controlling man, she has been robbed of her decision-making freedom, and she will naturally defer to us to make decisions for her. Our role is to empower her to reclaim her ability to make choices and to learn to make the hard decisions she needs to make.

5. Not Insisting on the Fruits of Repentance Before Initiating Reconciliation

It is tempting to encourage reconciliation once we see a husband begin to own his problems and want to change. We're encouraged that his eyes have been opened and change is taking place. Yet as we learned in chapters 12 and 13, a change of heart is still a long way from a change in habit. We want to see evidence of repentance in actions and actions over time and don't want this couple to fall back into repeating their old destructive history, which will happen if new habits aren't in place.

Individuals and couples seeking help for their destructive marriage are often looking for a quick fix. They can also be very challenging, especially because progress can be so slow. Be sure to get plenty of your own support as well as case consultation as needed. These situations require great wisdom and a strong commitment to stay the course for true healing and restoration.

Notes

Chapter 1

1. Annie Dillard, *Pilgrim at Tinker Creek* (New York: HarperPerennial, 1998), 33.

Chapter 2

1. I speak about mutual caring, mutual honesty, and mutual respect more extensively in my book *The Emotionally Destructive Relationship: Seeing It, Stopping It, Surviving It* (Eugene, OR: Harvest House, 2007), 36–39.
2. Timothy Keller and Kathy Keller, *The Meaning of Marriage: Facing the Complexities of Commitment with the Wisdom of God* (New York: Dutton, 2011), 47.

Chapter 3

1. For more help in learning how to respond biblically to provocative marital situations, read my book *How to Act Right When Your Spouse Acts Wrong* (Colorado Springs: WaterBrook, 2001).
2. Ginny Nicarthy, *Getting Free* (Seattle: Seal Press, 1997), 286–7, which shows Albert Biderman's Chart of Coercion. (This chart may also be viewed at the website in the next note.)
3. To learn more about techniques used on prisoners of war, including Albert Biderman's Chart of Coercion, see *Amnesty International Report on Torture* (New York: Farrar, Straus and Giroux, 1975), 53, or Center for the Study of Human Rights in the

Americas, "Military Training Materials," http://humanrights
.ucdavis.edu/projects/the-guantanamo-testimonials-project
/testimonies/testimonies-of-the-defense-department/military
-training-materials.

4. Oswald Chambers, *My Utmost for His Highest: Selections for the Year* (Uhrichsville, OH: Barbour, 1987), 154.

5. To read more about changing a destructive dance with someone, see chapter 6 of my book *The Emotionally Destructive Relationship.*

6. Scripture is clear that indifference is sin. 1 Timothy 5:8 says that those who don't show care for family members are worse than unbelievers. 1 John 3:17–19 says that love is demonstrated by loving actions, not just words. The story of the good Samaritan illustrates that Jesus values compassion and care and regards indifference to someone's suffering or pain as sin (Luke 10:25–37).

7. "Ignoring someone over time conveys the message 'you don't exist' and may be one of the most unrecognized yet serious forms of emotional abuse (Sackett & Saunders, 1999)." *The Popular Encyclopedia of Christian Counseling: An Indispensible Tool for Helping People with Their Problems,* ed. Dr. Tim Clinton and Dr. Ron Hawkins (Eugene, OR: Harvest House, 2011), 271.

8. The commentary I consulted regarding this story remarked, "It is our duty [as Christians] to speak out and take action in relation to painful subjects when anything can be done to effect an improvement. Evils are allowed to go unchecked because a false modesty dreads to speak of them. The men and women who overcome this and bravely advocate unpopular questions should be treated with all honour by the Christian Church. If the Christian does nothing to check the vicious practices and corrupt institutions which surround him, he becomes responsible

for their continued existence." H. D. M. Spence-Jones, ed., *The Pulpit Commentary: Judges* (Bellingham, WA: Logos Research Systems, 2004,) 197–8.

9. See the discussion of lust by Marnie C. Ferree and Mark R. Laaser, "Sexual Sin and Personal Holiness," in *The Soul Care Bible,* ed. Tim Clinton, Edward Hindson, and George Ohlschlager (Nashville: Thomas Nelson, 2001), 1582. They defined lust as "the desire to gratify sexual needs in purely physical ways outside the spiritual and emotional commitment of marriage." Is it not lust to require a wife to be sexually available to gratify her husband's physical needs when there is no spiritual or emotional commitment to her well-being or welfare as his wife?

10. Bill Farrel and Pam Farrel, *The 10 Best Decisions a Single Can Make: Embracing All God Has for You* (Eugene, OR: Harvest House, 2011), 126.

Chapter 4

1. The *Tyndale Bible Dictionary* says, "The essence of covenant is to be found in a particular kind of relationship between persons. Mutual obligations characterize that kind of relationship. Thus a covenant relationship is not merely a mutual acquaintance but a commitment to responsibility and action. A key word in Scripture to describe that commitment is 'faithfulness,' acted out in a context of abiding friendship.… To appreciate the many OT laws on marriage and divorce, one must understand that marriage itself was a covenant relationship (Mal 2:14). The solemn promises exchanged by a man and woman became their covenant obligations. Faithfulness to those promises brought marital blessing (cf. Ps 128; Prv 18:22); violation brought a curse." Walter A. Elwell

and Philip W. Comfort, eds., *Tyndale Bible Dictionary,* Tyndale Reference Library (Wheaton, IL: Tyndale, 2001), 323.

In another source, various types of covenants are explained. According to Old Testament scholar J. Barton Payne, marriage is a parity covenant. A parity covenant is a contract between equal parties—an agreement entered into that includes promises to each other. Each party was expected to keep his or her promises and to be loyal to the covenant, but sometimes that did not happen. And when it didn't, the covenant was broken, considered null and void. Severe consequences could follow one breaking his covenant agreement. J. B. Payne, "Covenant (in the Old Testament)," from *The Zondervan Pictorial Encyclopedia of the Bible, Vol. 1,* Merrill C. Tenney, ed., (Grand Rapids, MI: Zondervan, 1976), 1001–2. Joe M. Sprinkle, "Old Testament Perspectives on Divorce and Remarriage," *Journal of the Evangelical Theological Society* 40, no. 4 (December 1997): 546.

Other parity covenants included individuals such as David and Jonathan (see 1 Samuel 18:3–4), households such as Jacob and the brethren of Laban (see Genesis 31:43–44), groups such as the Amorites of Hebron and Abraham (see Genesis 14:13), and even whole nations such as Edom and its confederates (see Obadiah1:7).

2. Jesus stopped his public ministry among the people and left Jerusalem because he knew the leaders plotted to kill him (see John 11:53–54).

3. The rules and regulations around Sabbath keeping are a very good illustration of how the Pharisees tried to enforce a rigid legalistic application to God's principles while missing the more important truths of God's heart. When we legalistically apply a single verse like "I hate divorce" and make an entire statement

about whether or not someone can leave a destructive marriage, I think we're guilty of the same error that the Pharisees made concerning the Sabbath.

4. See chapter 2 of my book *The Emotionally Destructive Relationship* for more information on the effects of living with a destructive person. Also look at Daniel Goleman's book *Social Intelligence* (New York: Bantam Dell, 2006) to see research on the effect of toxic people and emotions on our well-being.

5. For more information on developing a safety plan in an abusive relationship, visit your local domestic-violence support group, or call 1-800-799-SAFE (7233) to talk to a trained abuse counselor, or go to appendix A for other resources.

Chapter 6

1. Carolyn Custis James, *Lost Women of the Bible: Finding Strength and Significance Through Their Stories* (Grand Rapids, MI: Zondervan, 2005), 36.

2. Peter cautions church leaders, "Don't lord it over the people assigned to your care, but lead them by your own good example" (1 Peter 5:3, NLT). In the Old Testament, God warned the Jews not to rule over their slaves with rigor (see Leviticus 25:43, NKJV).

Chapter 8

1. I used Matthew 18:15–17 to explain the process of how to speak up, stand up, and step back from an emotionally destructive person in chapter 9 of my book *The Emotionally Destructive Relationship.* Some people wrote and commented that their church leadership told them that Matthew 18 is not applicable to marriage relationships but only to relationships within the church.

How can that be? Does Jesus have a lower standard for marriage than other relationships in the church? Scripture clearly teaches God has set a higher standard for the way spouses treat one another. Only husbands are commanded to love as Christ loves the church (see Ephesians 5:25–26).

Matthew 18 does indicate witnesses are to be a part of the confrontation process if someone refuses to listen, and that the church should become involved when a person refuses to repent. Emotionally destructive marriages may have some witnesses in the form of other family members and children, but in addition, witnesses may include financial documents, police reports, and photographs of injuries to one's body or property. These witnesses can be used to help church leaders implement the third step of the confrontation process.

If the husband is not a believer, church leaders can still speak with him in the hopes of bringing him to Christ, but since he has not placed himself under their authority, the consequences of church discipline are not applicable. There are instances where the witnesses of legal authorities and church authorities can join together for a powerful intervention. Counseling is usually preferred to jail when those are one's only options.

2. The Old Testament books of Isaiah and Jeremiah are full of examples of God inviting people into repentance, talking to them, pleading with them, but also giving them consequences and distancing himself from those people in the hopes that they would wake up and repent. (Read Jeremiah 1–4 for starters.) Jeremiah 16:5 is particularly strong where the Lord says, "I have removed my protection and peace from them. I have taken away my unfailing love and my mercy" (NLT). Why, they ask? "What

have we done to deserve such treatment?" (verse 10, NLT). The Lord responds, "You stubbornly follow your own evil desires and refuse to listen to me" (verse 12, NLT).

In John 3:16, it says "God so loved the world" (unconditional love), but it also says in John 3:36, "Whoever believes in the Son has eternal life; whoever does not obey the Son shall not see life, but the wrath of God remains on him" (conditional relationship).

Chapter 9

1. For an interesting parallel, read through Jeremiah 7. The people of God thought that just because the temple was in Jerusalem, they would continue to receive God's blessings in spite of their wicked ways. God repeatedly spoke to Israel about her idolatry and indifference, but she would not listen. Eventually God withdrew his blessings and his relationship with them. Jeremiah 7:19 says, "Most of all, they hurt themselves, to their own shame" (NLT). Your husband may believe he's entitled to all the blessings of marriage while treating you abusively and violating his marital promises. That is not true, and to collude with his self-deceit is enabling his delusional thinking to remain unchallenged.

Chapter 10

1. You can also learn how to speak up with difficult people in chapter 8 of my book *The Emotionally Destructive Relationship*.

2. When Queen Esther wanted to confront the king with Haman's sin, she invited him for dinner. But while there, she didn't feel that the timing was right. When the king asked her what she wanted, she asked him to come back for dinner the next night. It was then Esther told the king what Haman had done (see Esther 5).

3. In Jeremiah 5:11–19, God implemented the gift of consequences
   to help the people of Israel and Judah wake up and change their
   ways. In Deuteronomy 28–30, God outlines the requirements for
   blessings and the consequences of disobedience.

4. The standard answer women often hear from biblical counselors
   and pastors on this subject is that the Bible says that a wife may
   not withhold herself sexually from her husband, citing 1 Corinthians 7. But what are we saying to a woman by this counsel? Are
   we saying that her husband's sexual needs (or desires) are more
   important to God than her emotional well-being? Are we telling
   her that God calls her to meet her husband's sexual needs regardless of the damage he's done to her spirit or their relationship? Are
   we telling her that God says she never has a choice? she is to be
   available sexually no matter what?

   That is a horrible and incorrect picture of God. When we
   paint that picture of God, we are telling a woman that God
   values a man's sexual needs and desires more than a woman's
   needs for love and safety, and this is not the truth. God cares
   equally for both individuals in a marriage and for the relationship itself. See my article "Does God Value Sex More than
   Safety?" at www.leslievernick.com/the-emotionally-destructive
   -marriage.

5. Henry Cloud, *Necessary Endings: The Employees, Businesses, and
   Relationships That All of Us Have to Give Up In Order to Move
   Forward* (New York: HarperCollins, 2010), 144.

6. In my earlier book *The Emotionally Destructive Relationship,*
   I list seven pervasive sins of the heart that are chronic in
   destructive relationship patterns. They are pride, anger, envy,
   selfishness, laziness, fear, and evil. Also Lundy Bancroft has
   written an excellent book *Why Does He Do That? Inside the*

Minds of Angry and Controlling Men (New York: Berkley, 2002), which is very helpful to understand more of the reasons behind someone's behavior.

7. David Adams, "Certified Batterer Intervention Programs," paper adapted and updated from "Treatment for Batterers," *Clinics in Family Practice* 5, no. 1 (May 2003): 159–76.

8. By safe, I do not just mean physical safety. You must also be safe emotionally, mentally, sexually, financially, and spiritually.

Chapter 11

1. The entire discussion and debate concerning whether divorce and remarriage are biblically permissible is exhaustive and beyond the scope of this book. To read a brief summary of the three main viewpoints held by conservative Christians, go to www.leslievernick.com/the-emotionally-destructive-marriage and read my article "Is Divorce a Biblical Option in Destructive Marriage?" Also read David Instone-Brewer's article "What God Has Joined: What Does the Bible Really Teach About Divorce?," *Christianity Today* 51, no. 10 (October 2007), www.christianity today.com/ct/2007/october/20.26.html, and his book *Divorce and Remarriage in the Bible: The Social and Literary Context* (Grand Rapids, MI: Eerdmans, 2002).

2. Catherine Clark Kroeger, "Divorce, Domestic Violence and Saddleback Church," *PASCH Newsletter*, January/February 2009, 4–5.

3. National Institute of Mental Health, "Women and Depression," Psych Central, last modified January 30, 2013, http://psychcentral .com/lib/2007/women-and-depression.

4. Daniel Goleman, *Social Intelligence: The New Science of Human Relationships* (New York: Bantam Dell, 2006), 5.

5. Project Making Medicine, Center on Child Abuse and Neglect, "The Effects of Domestic Violence on Children" (Oklahoma City: University of Oklahoma Health Sciences Center, 2005), 5, http://ktik-nsn.gov/documents/effects_dv_children.pdf.

6. Wade F. Horn, "Putting Children Back at the Center of Things" *Fatherhood Today* 4, no. 4 (Winter 2000): 3. For more information on the long-term effects of divorce on children, see Judith S. Wallerstein, Julia M. Lewis, and Sandra Blakeslee, *The Unexpected Legacy of Divorce: The 25 Year Landmark Study* (New York: Hyperion, 2000).

Chapter 12

1. A study in contrasts in the Old Testament illustrates this important truth. Samuel the prophet confronted King Saul when he deliberately disobeyed the Lord's instructions. Saul responded with denial and deceit. Samuel was brokenhearted over Saul's pride and lack of repentance. Saul made a halfhearted attempt to show Samuel that he repented with a few superficial changes. God knew Saul was not repentant and removed Saul's anointing as king. Saul mourned the consequences, but he did not mourn over his sin against God. (Read 1 Samuel 15–16 for the story.)

   King David also sinned when he abused his power and ordered Bathsheba to his bed. To make matters worse, when Bathsheba turned up pregnant, he murdered her husband, Uriah, to avoid being found out. When Nathan the prophet confronted David with his sin, David repented. He expressed a broken and contrite heart. There were still consequences, but David took responsibility and willingly accepted them as from the Lord. (Read 2 Samuel 11–12 for the story, and Psalm 51 to see David's change of heart.)

2. Jesus said that Moses allowed divorce because of the hardness of their hearts (see Matthew 19:8).

3. There are many biblical references to making amends and the laws of restitution by someone who has injured another, whether physically, financially, or otherwise. A few are found in Exodus 21–22, Numbers 5:7, Leviticus 6:1–5, and Ephesians 4:28.

4. In 1 Samuel 26:17–27:1, Saul told David he was sorry and that he was wrong (see 26:21). He assured David that he would not seek his life again, but his words meant nothing. His actions showed otherwise.

5. François Fénelon, *Christian Perfection: Devotional Reflections on the Christian Life by a Seventeenth-Century Mystic* (Minneapolis: Bethany Fellowship, 1975), 3.

6. God wants us to recognize the lies we tell ourselves and listen to God's truth (see Amos 2:4, Isaiah 30:9–10, Hosea 12:1, Isaiah 44:20).

7. Proverbs 15:31–33 talks about the importance of listening to life-giving reproof, and when you listen to it, you gain wisdom.

8. *Alcoholics Anonymous,* 4th ed. (New York: Alcoholics Anonymous World Services, 2001), 25.

Discover Surprising Blessings in Your Struggles

Learn how to maintain your integrity and grow closer to God in the face of your spouse's wrongdoing: from petty irritants—like nagging or not listening—to betrayal and abuse.

Do you struggle with applying your faith to your daily trials? Discover the proven method that can bring you real spiritual growth—and change your life!